Drawn from Life

Drawn from Life

a figural response by Mary Kosowski

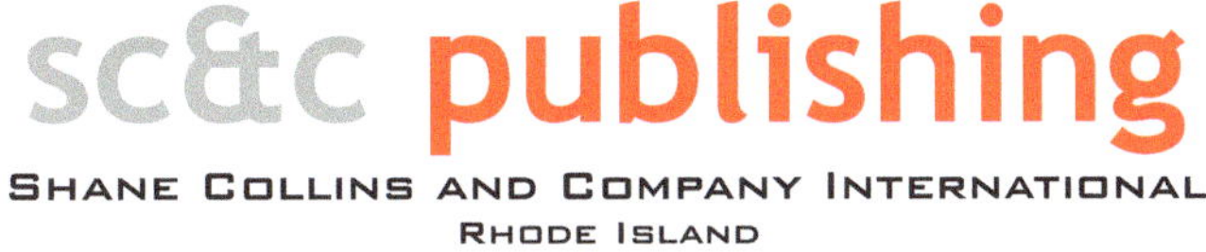

A Shane Collins and Company International Book
printed in accordance with Lulu Press

VOLUME ONE

ISBN 978-0-615-24701-4

Library of Congress Control Number: 2008905921

First Edition

To view more of Mary's work, please visit www.marykosowski.com

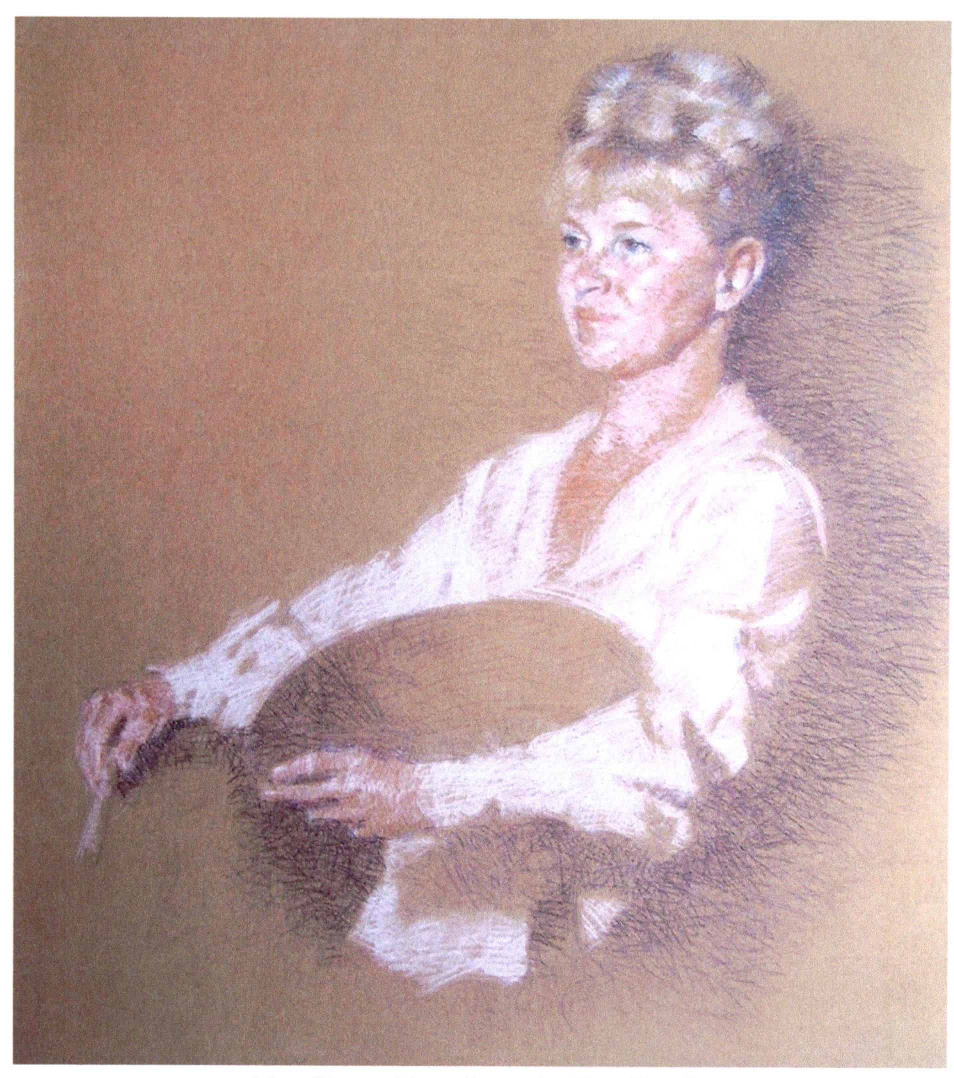

Mary Kosowski, as drawn by Tony Janello

Introduction

Drawing is the basic foundation of art, and my challenge and passion was the mastery of the human figure as I saw it. I'd like to believe that as Mary Cassatt was leaving this world, I was entering, perhaps with a bit of her gifts inherited – a lofty ambition!

My earliest recollections and happiest moments were always books, pencils, crayons and paper which were all hard to come by in our home. We were very poor, and I remember feeling so proud to bring home free coal, which sometimes fell (or was purposely shoveled) off of the nearby trains – the kind stokers were observant of the poverty of the children who hung around the railroad tracks. My older sisters were able to purchase nylon stockings from the city five-and-dime stores, and the lovely white blank inserts with each pair were treasured by me – ah, another sheet on which to draw. And then, once a month the postman delivered to the downstairs tenant a marvelous magazine, which I could hardly wait to look over before they returned from work and it disappeared into their apartment. I so anticipated the glorious covers of the *Saturday Evening Post*, illustrated by Norman Rockwell, for they made me wonder if I could ever emulate such draftsmanship. Who was this master I fell in love with? And so my pencils and I began our journey.

In elementary school, I was always picked to decorate the boards for holidays, which meant I could use the precious box of chalks, which held many, many colors that no one else could touch – and stay indoors, too, during recess, and even for a while during the teachers' lunch hour (if need be). I happily obliged throughout the years until high school, where I was made art editor of our class book and eventually obtained a four-year scholarship to attend the coveted Rhode Island School of Design (RISD). This was through the intercession of my art teachers: Eleanor Morse, Dorothy Johnson, and Mrs. Carpenter, who I gratefully acknowledge as finances were not available at home. But even so, my parents frowned upon a girl attending college when they were only going to get married and raise a family. However, because I agreed to work full-time, and was hired nights as a telephone operator for four years, they reluctantly gave permission.

I did graduate, and my first employment was as a curtain fabric designer at $25 a week. I married a RISD textile designer, had two daughters, and later worked as a designer of children's wear. From there I eventually became a teacher for twenty-four years in the public school system. At the same time, for several years I was in charge of the evening drawing classes in the continuing education department at the Rhode Island School of Design. In between all my jobs: as wife, mother, teacher, and pursuer of a Master's Degree I constantly sought out places to do what I enjoyed most – drawing and painting the model wherever and whenever I could.

Hundreds of drawings were produced, culminating in this book of some of my work. Every drawing was produced in one to twenty minutes maximum in order to capture the fluidity of the models pose. "Drawn from Life" is not a book about teaching. My hope is that my drawings will inspire you to develop in your own way and make you want to draw.

"Do whatever you do intensely."
- Robert Henri

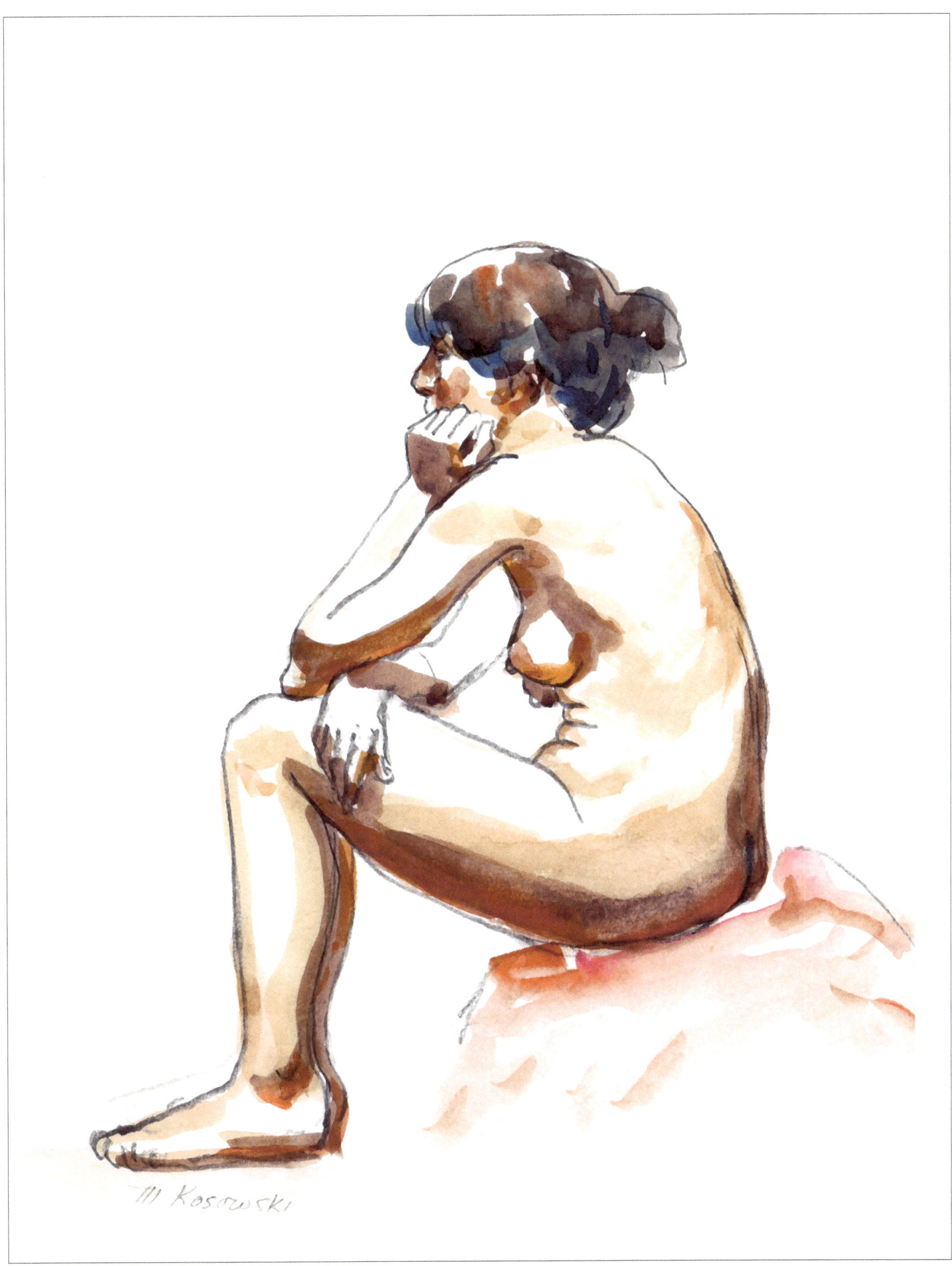
M Kosowski

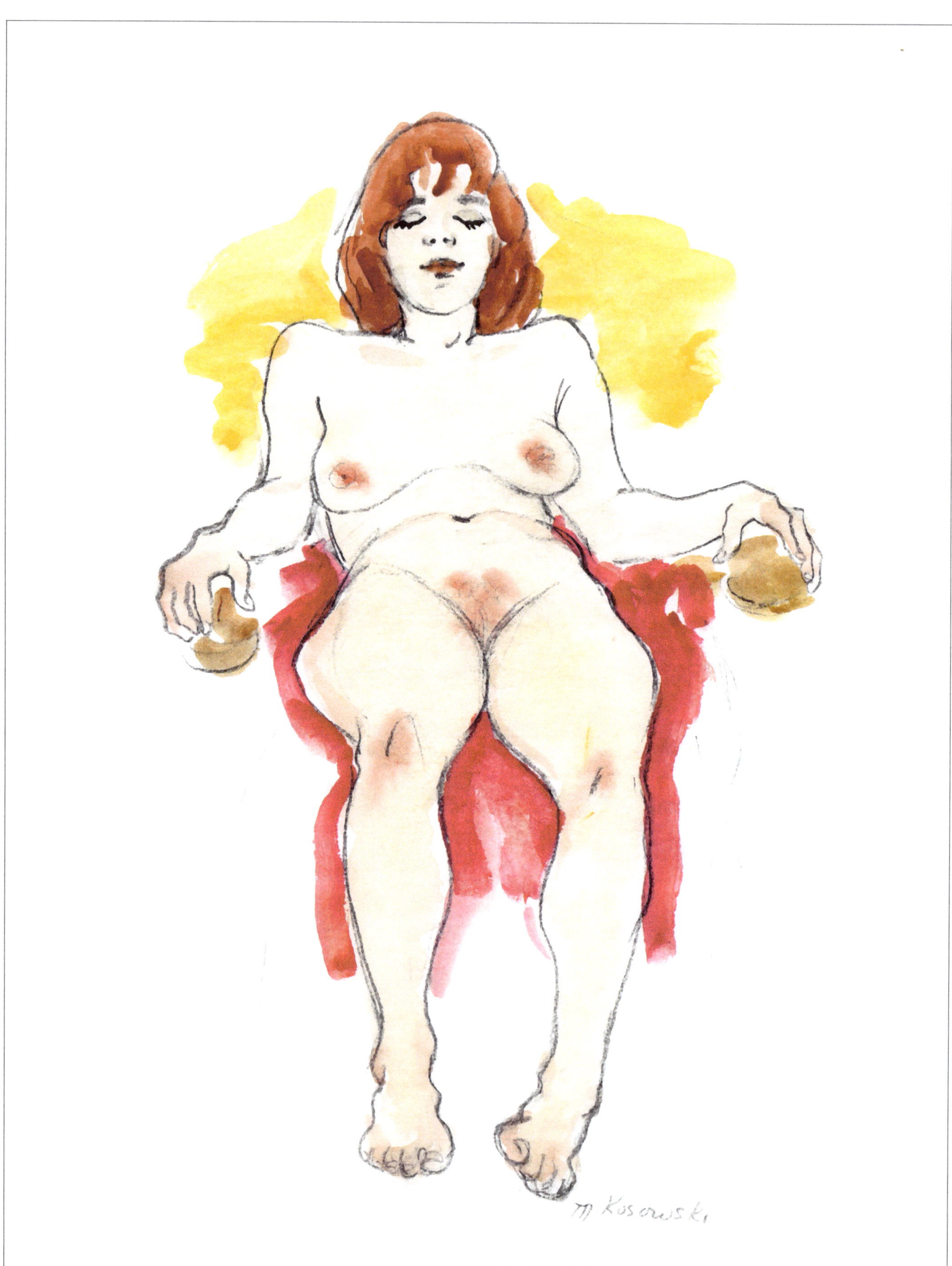
M Kosowski

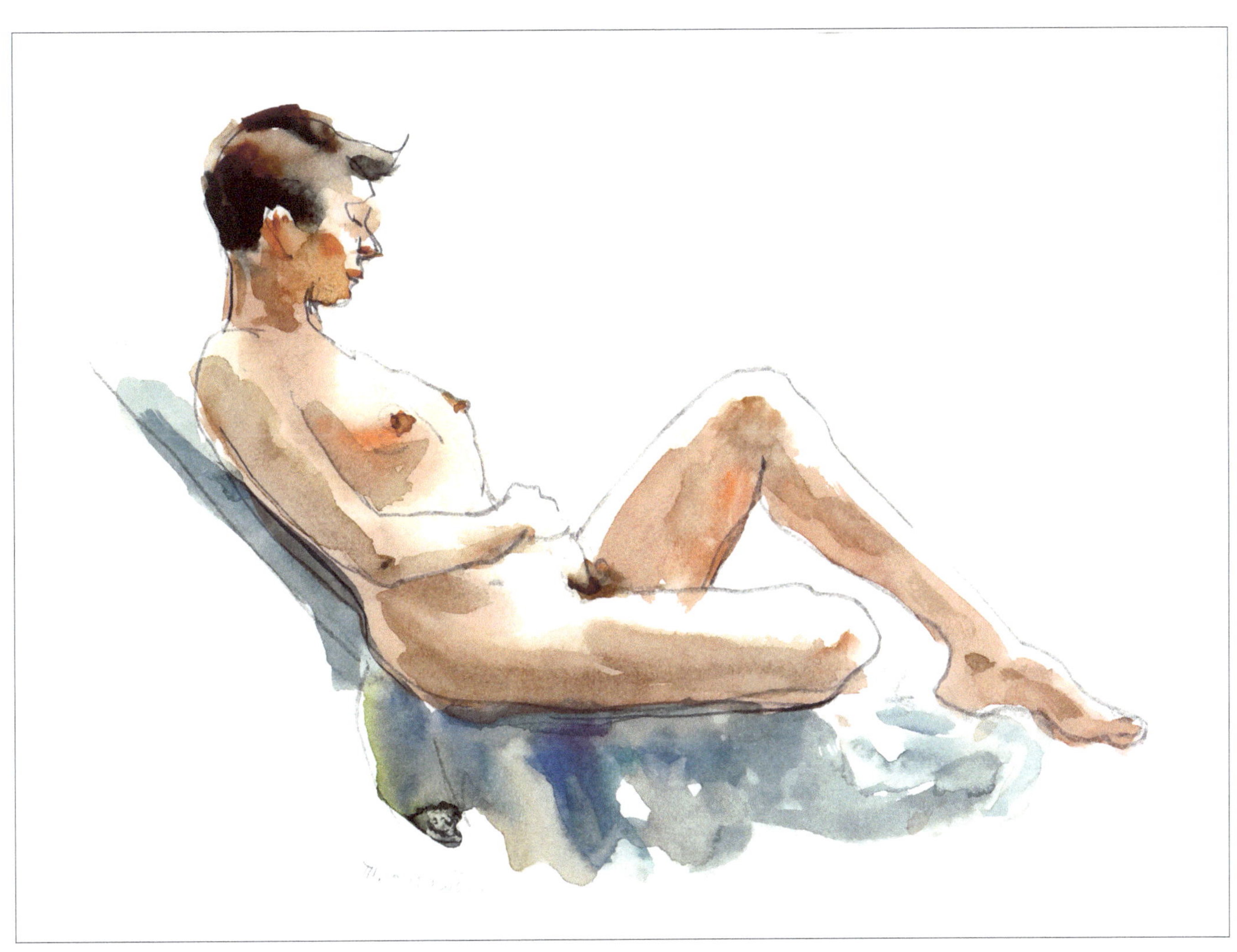

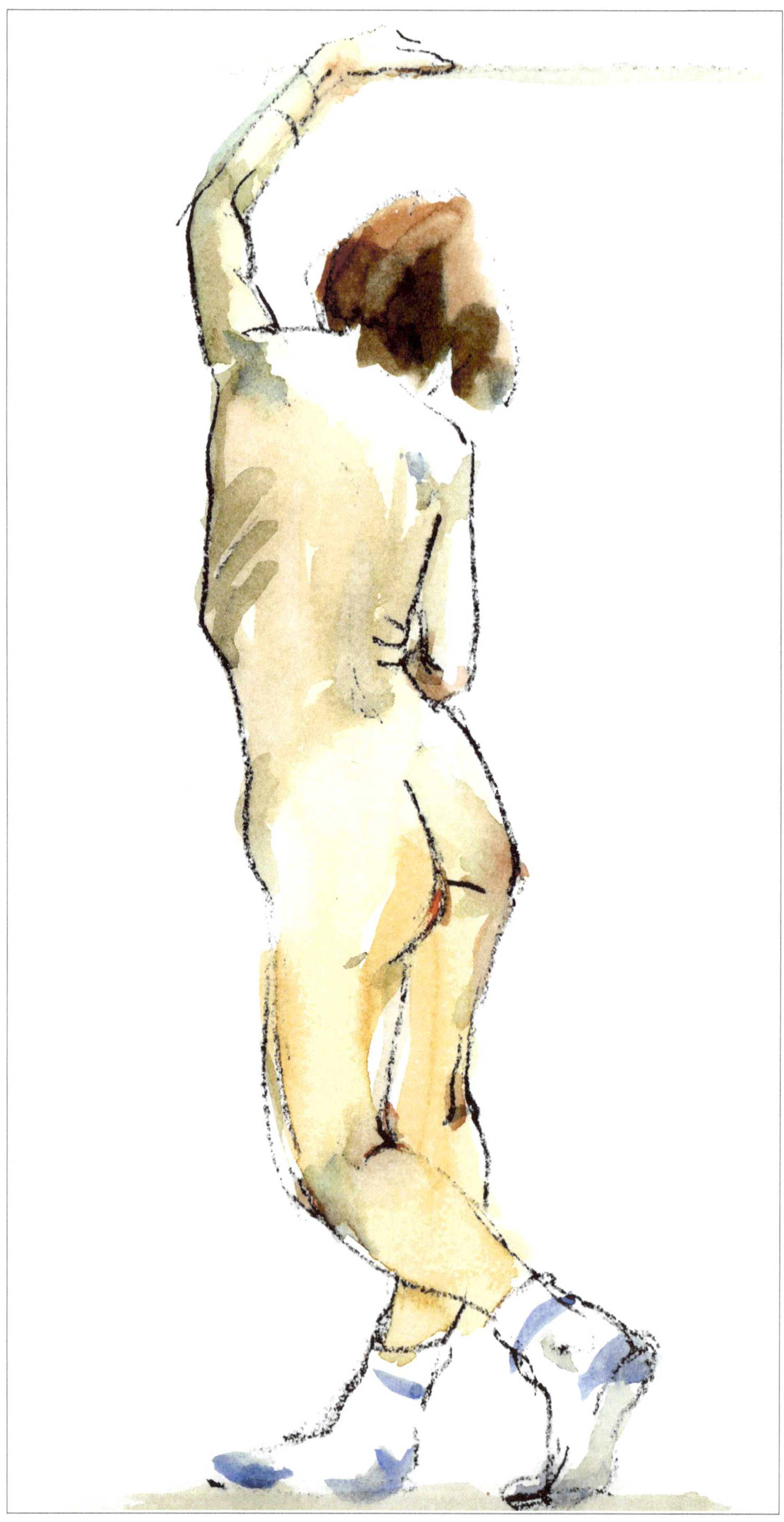

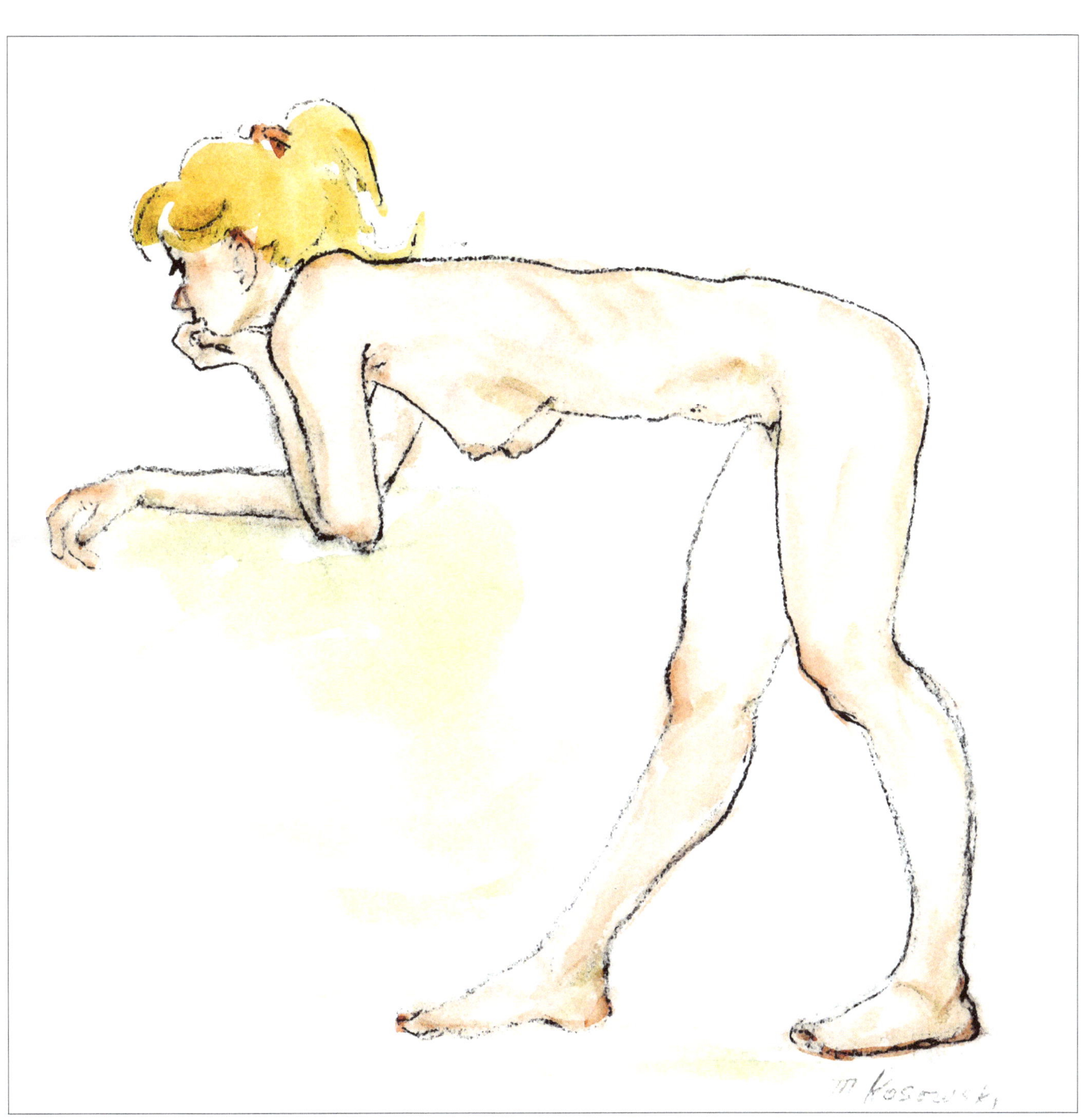

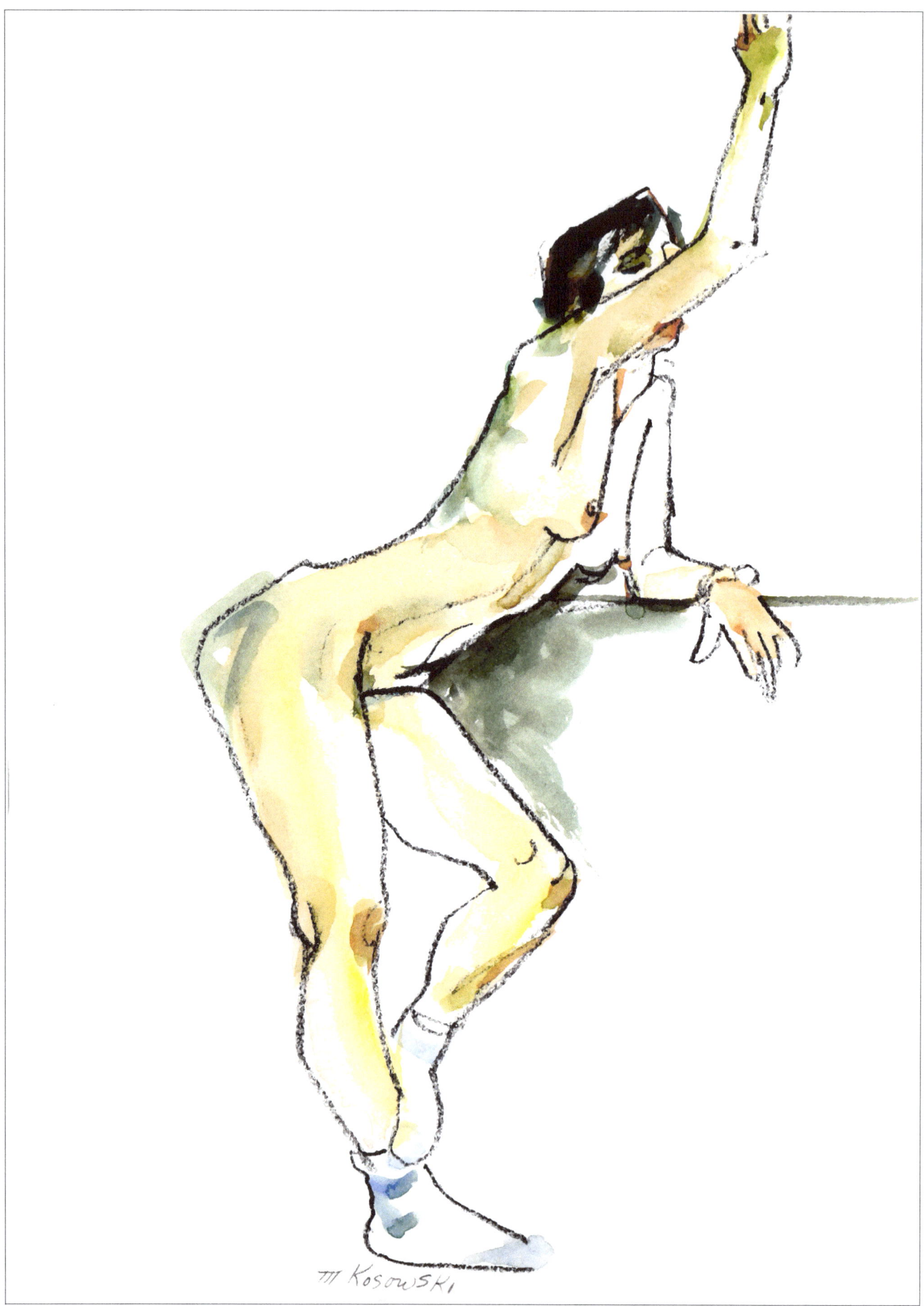
m Kosowski

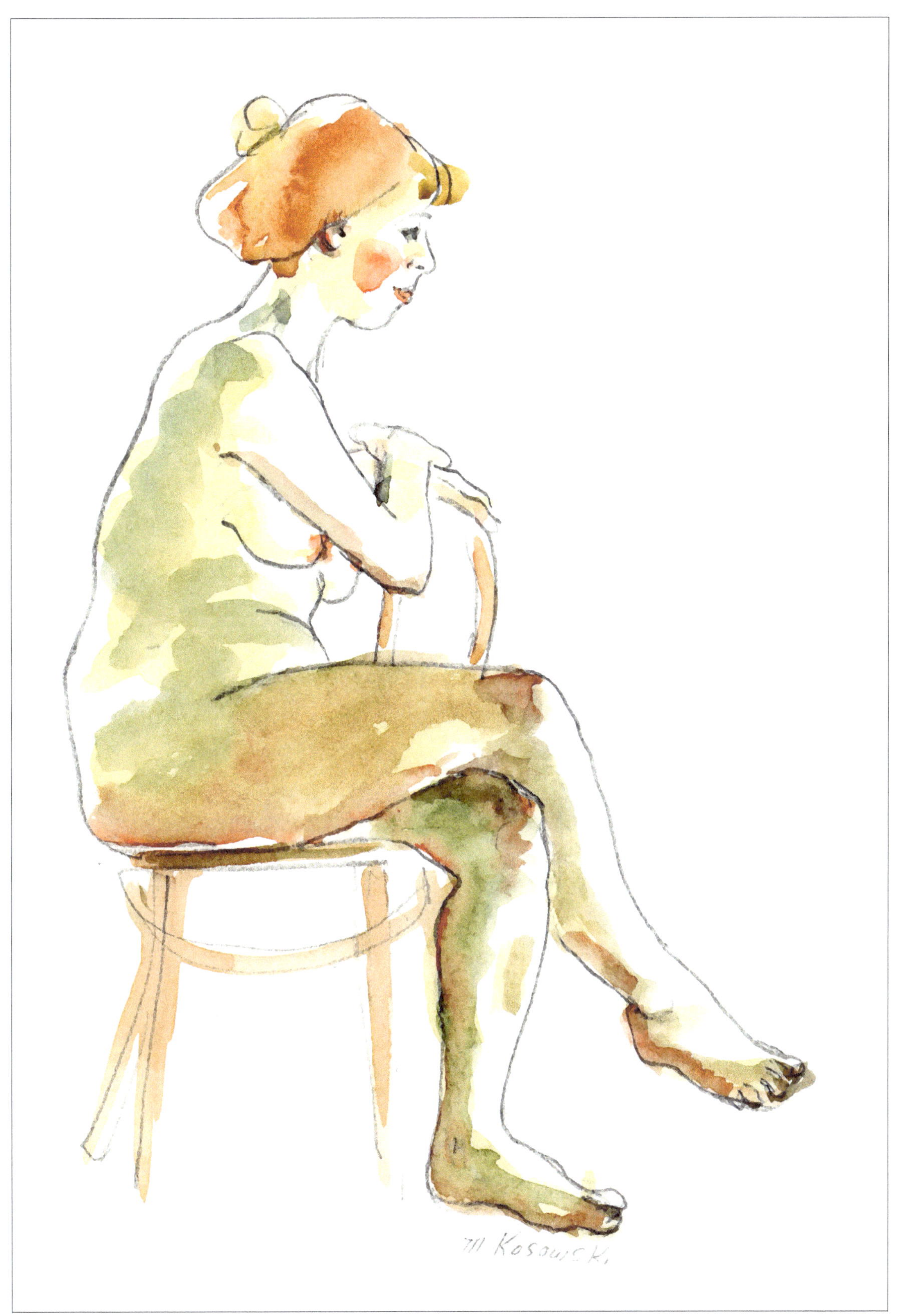

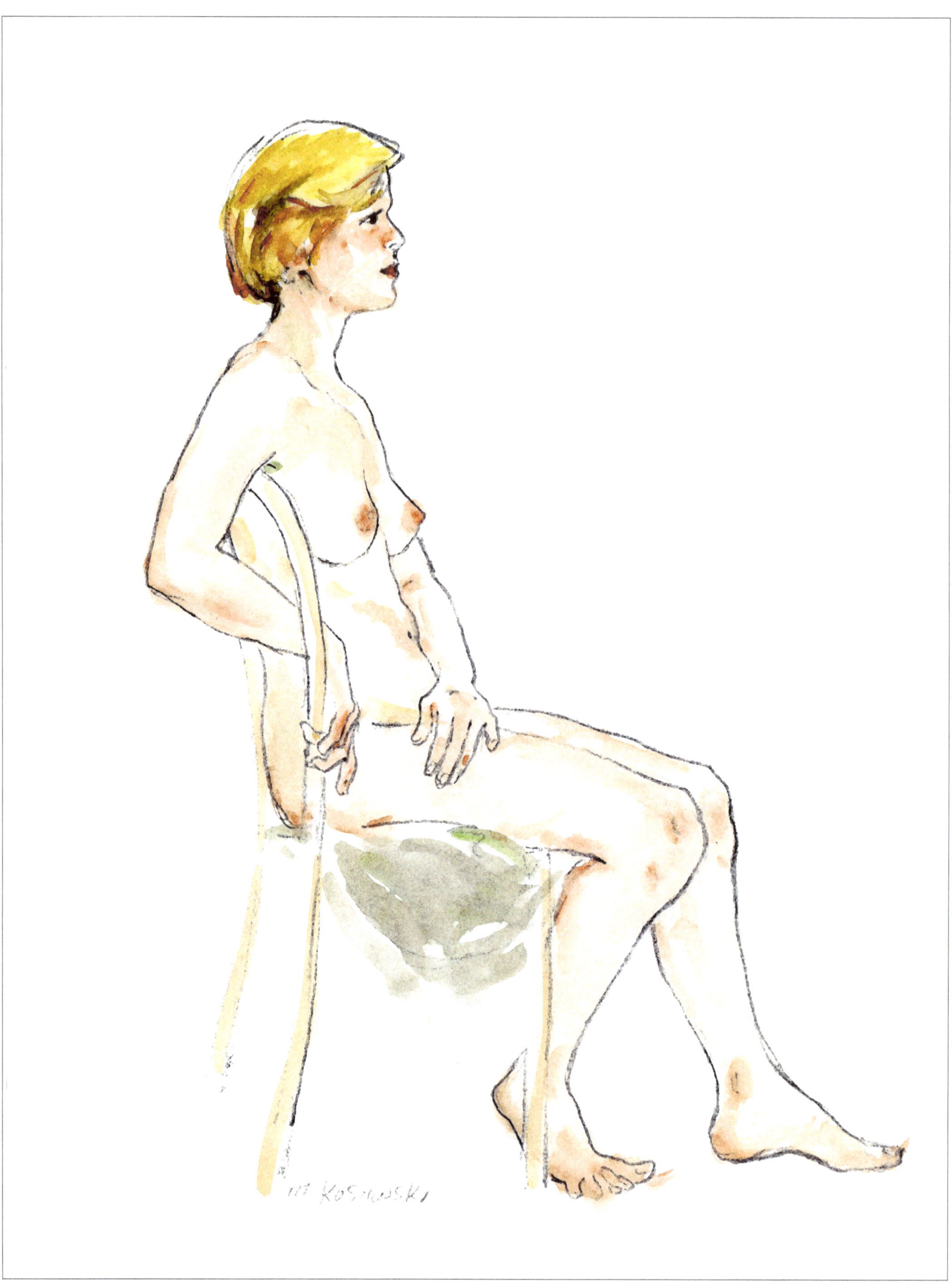

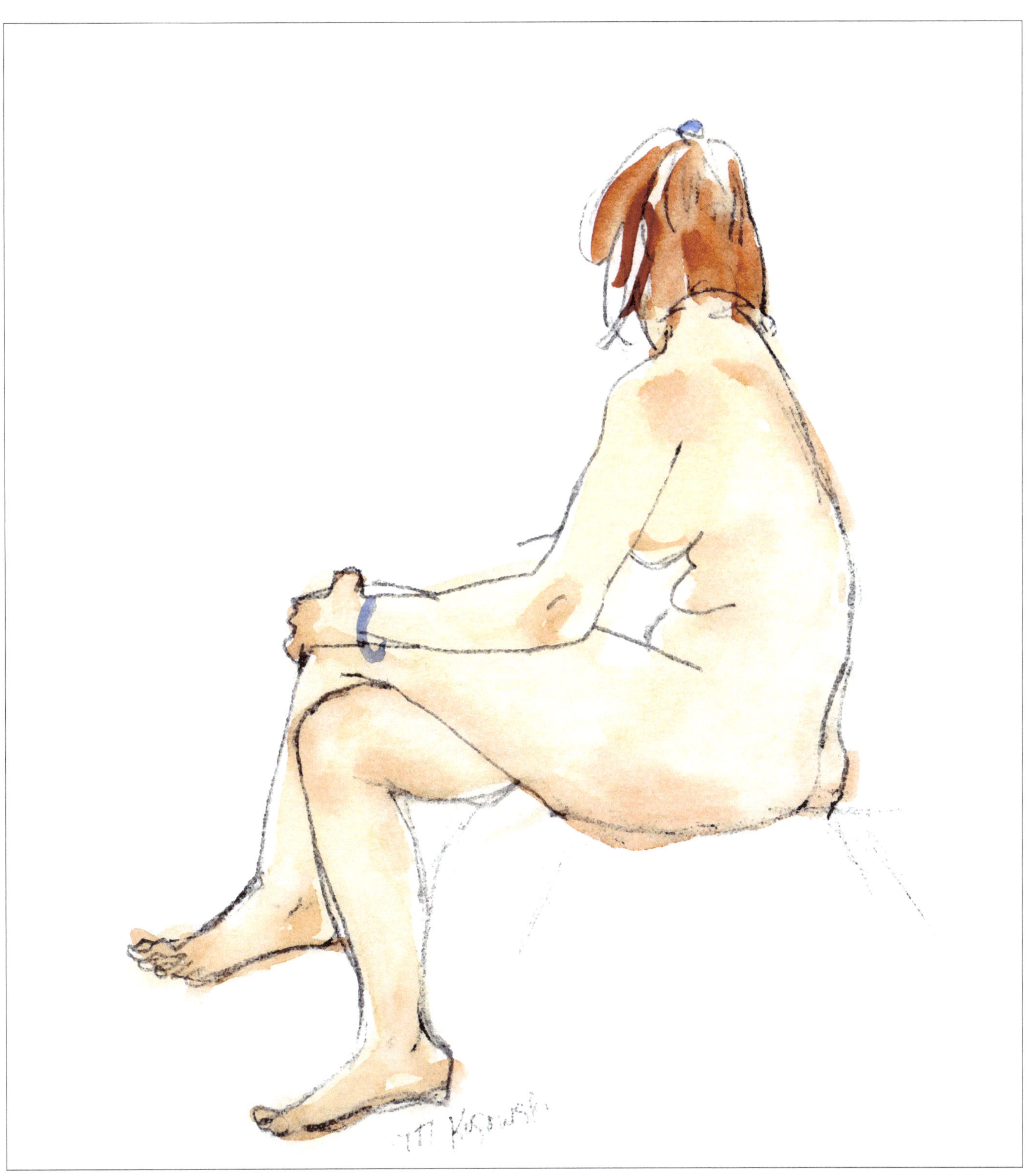

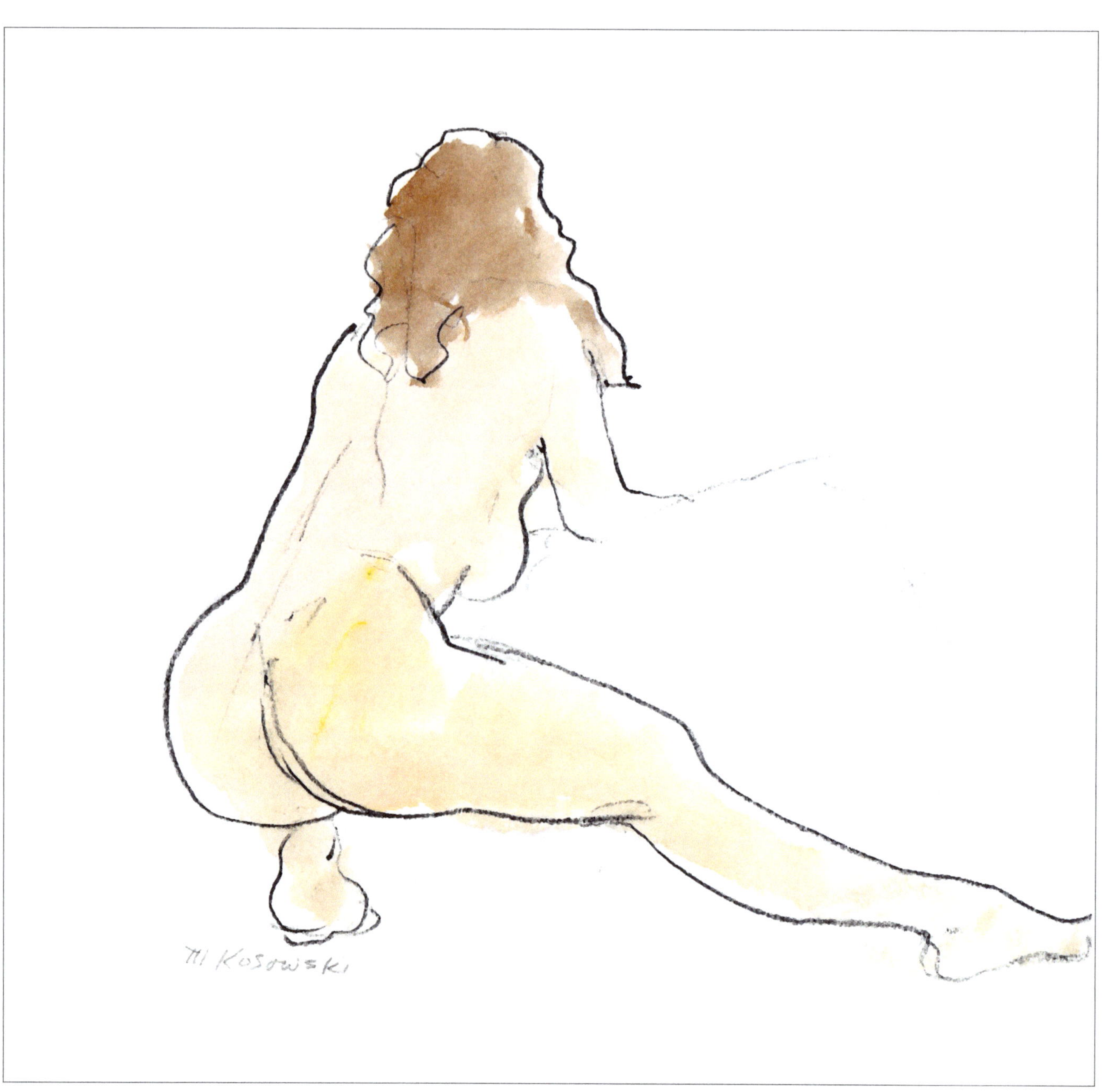
M KOSOWSKI

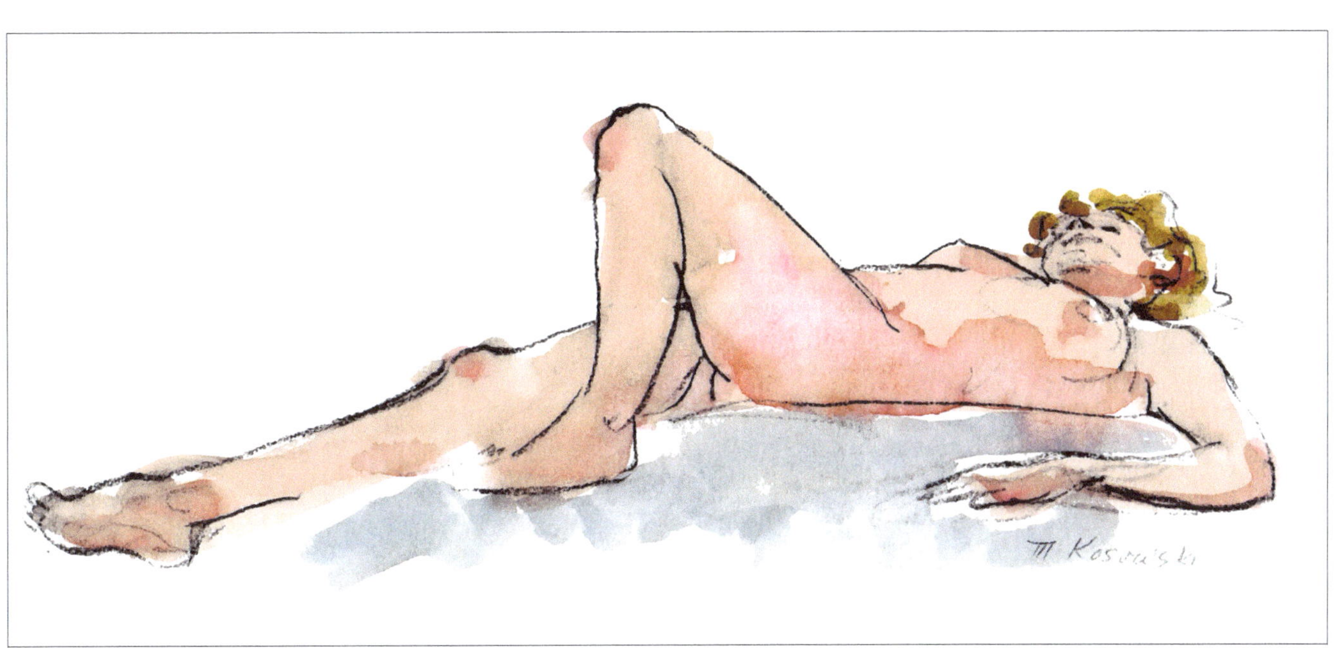

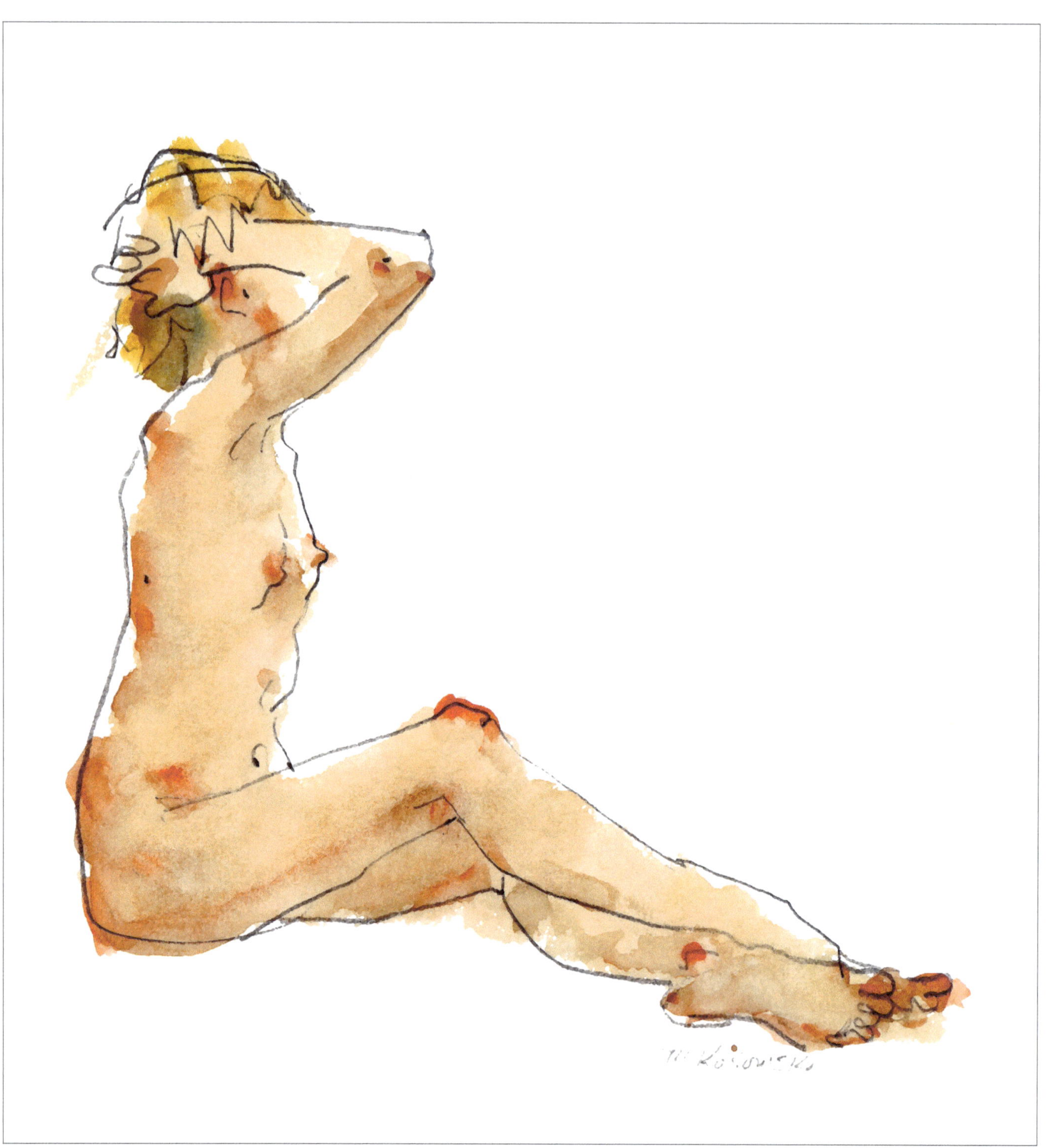

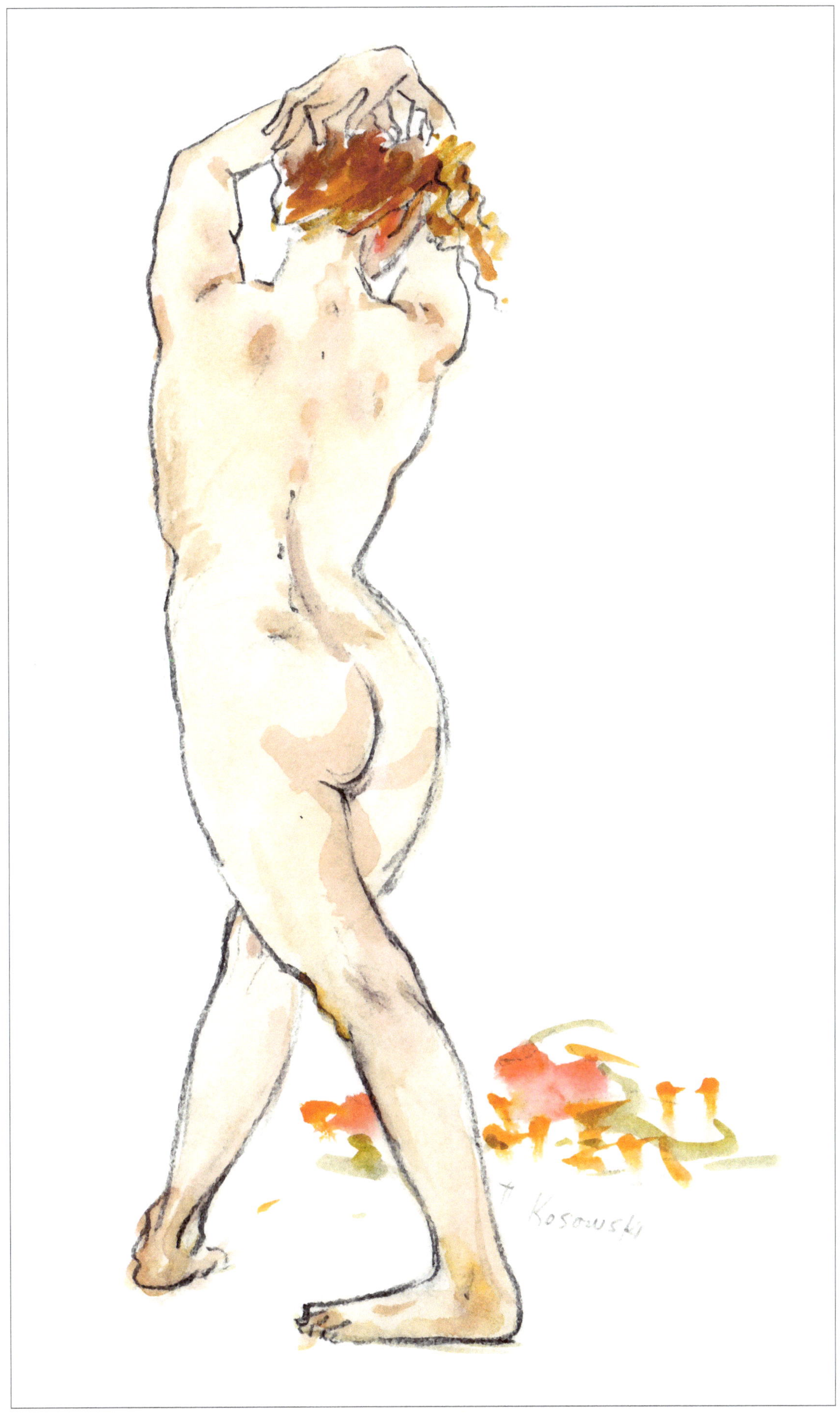
Kosowski

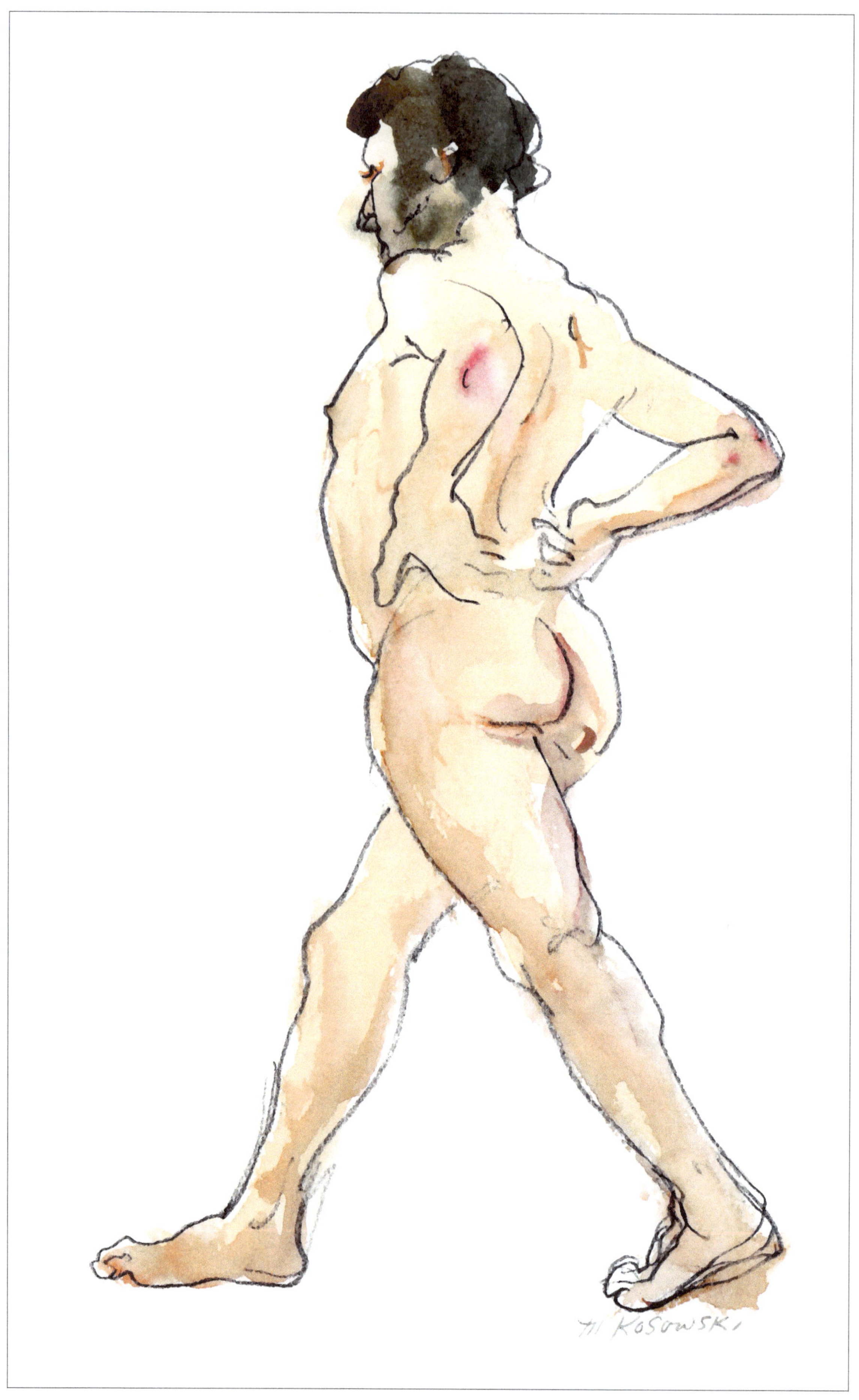
M KOSOWSKI

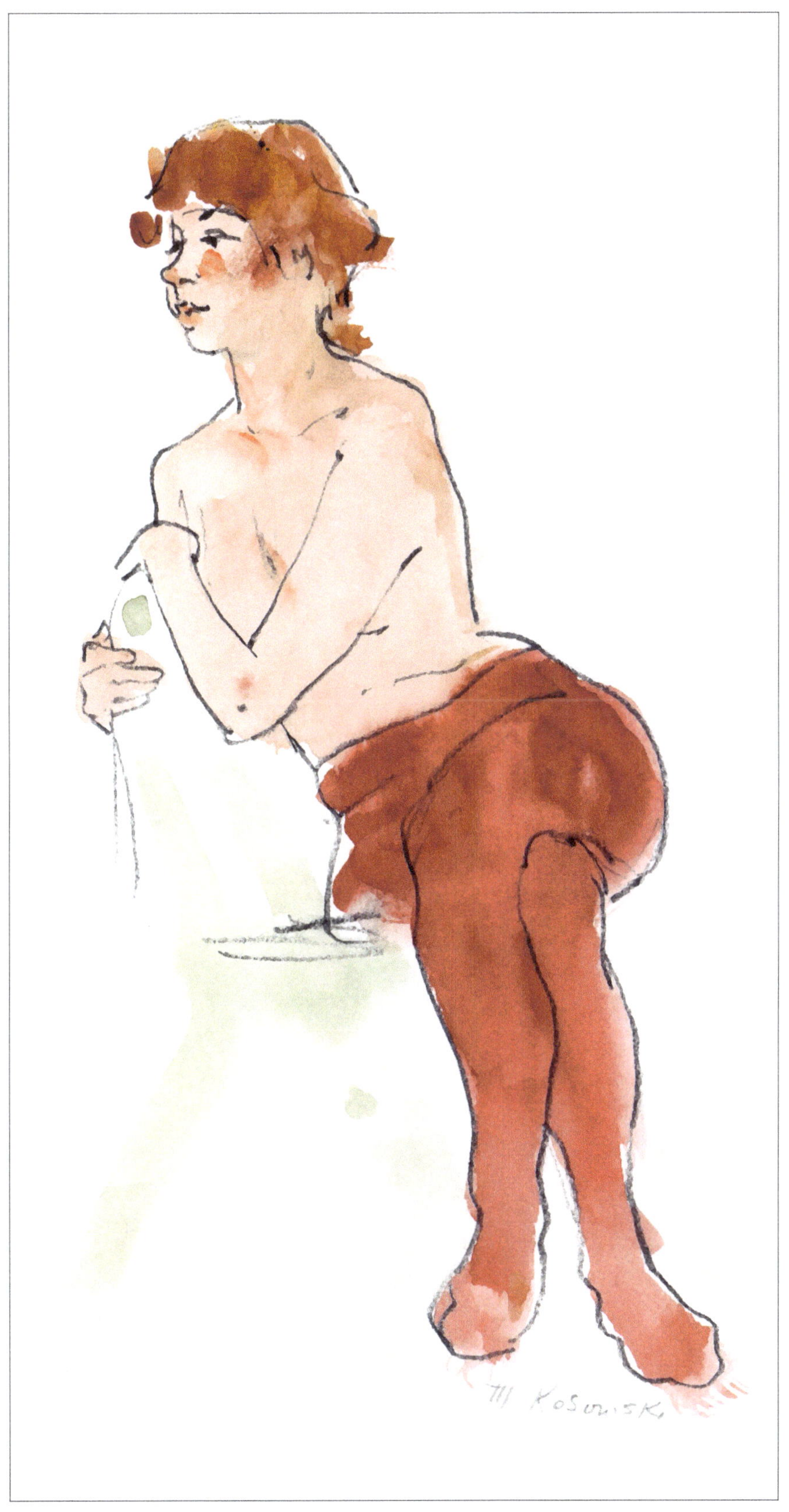

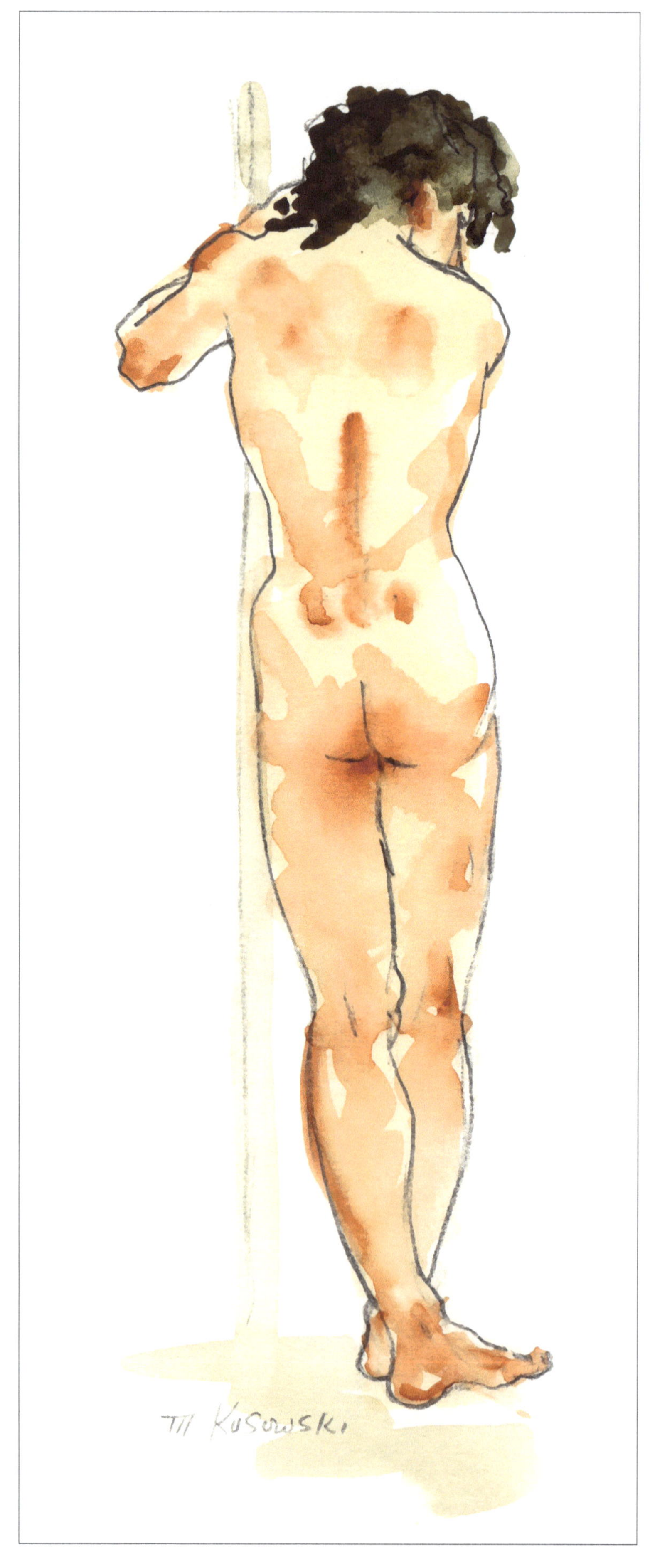

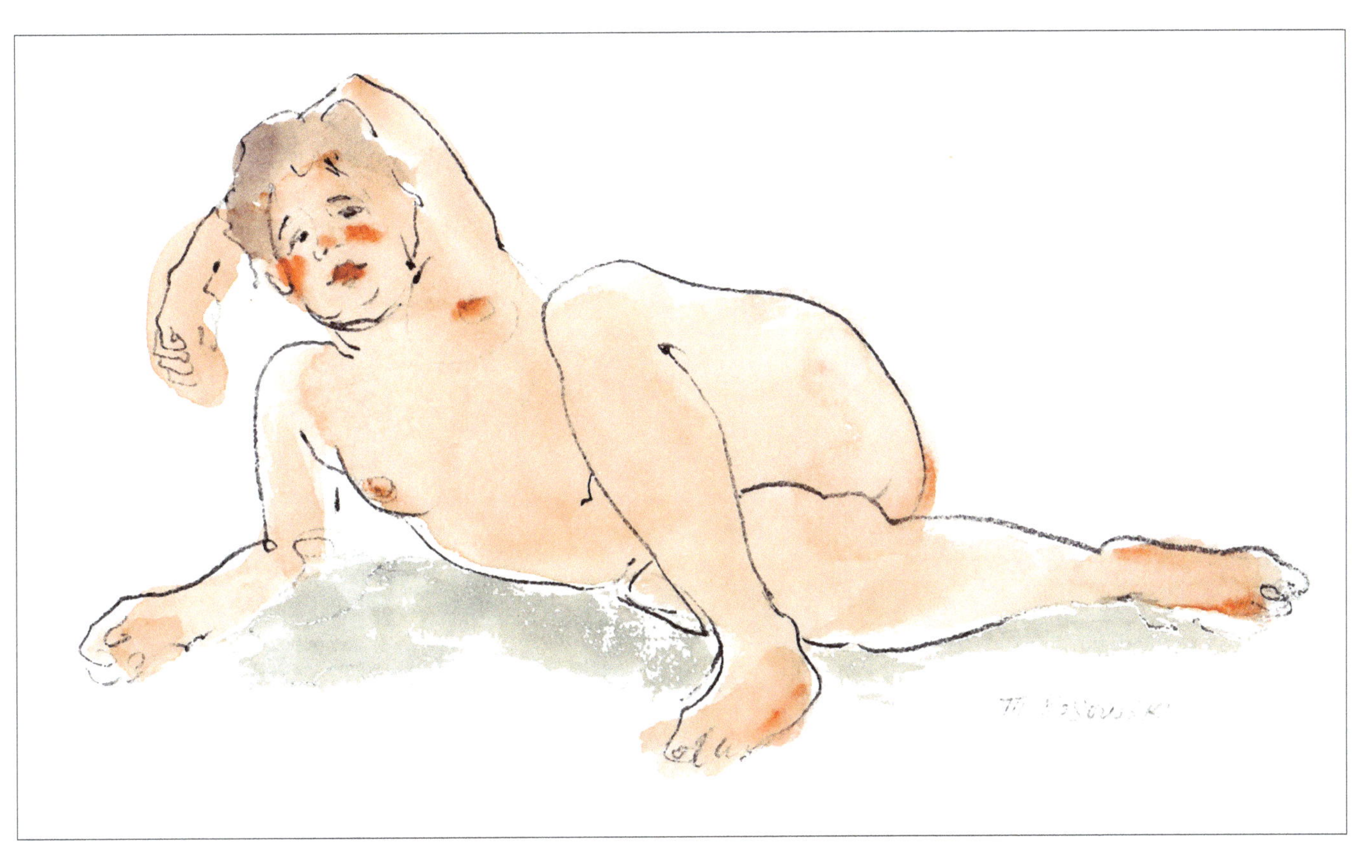

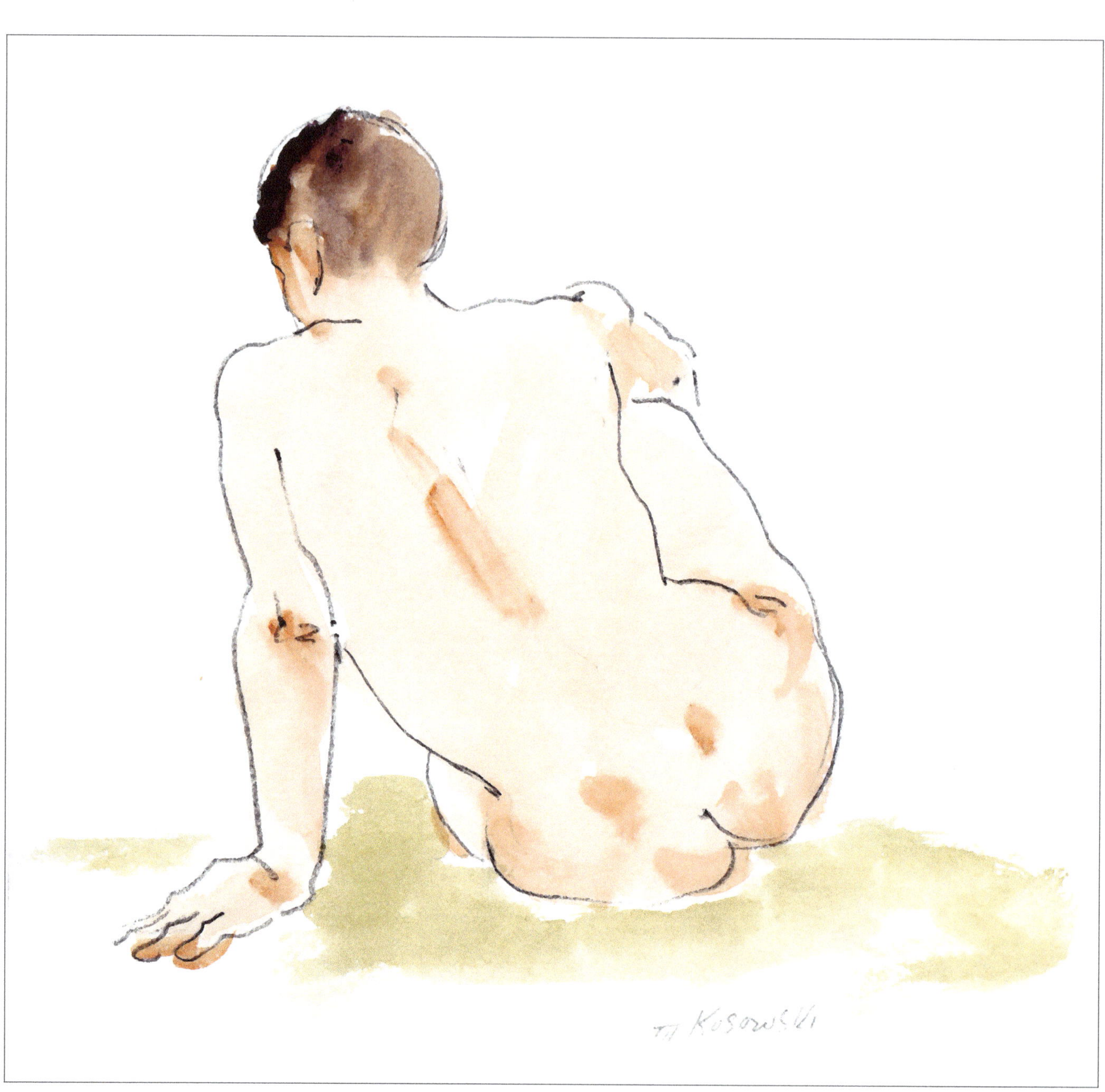

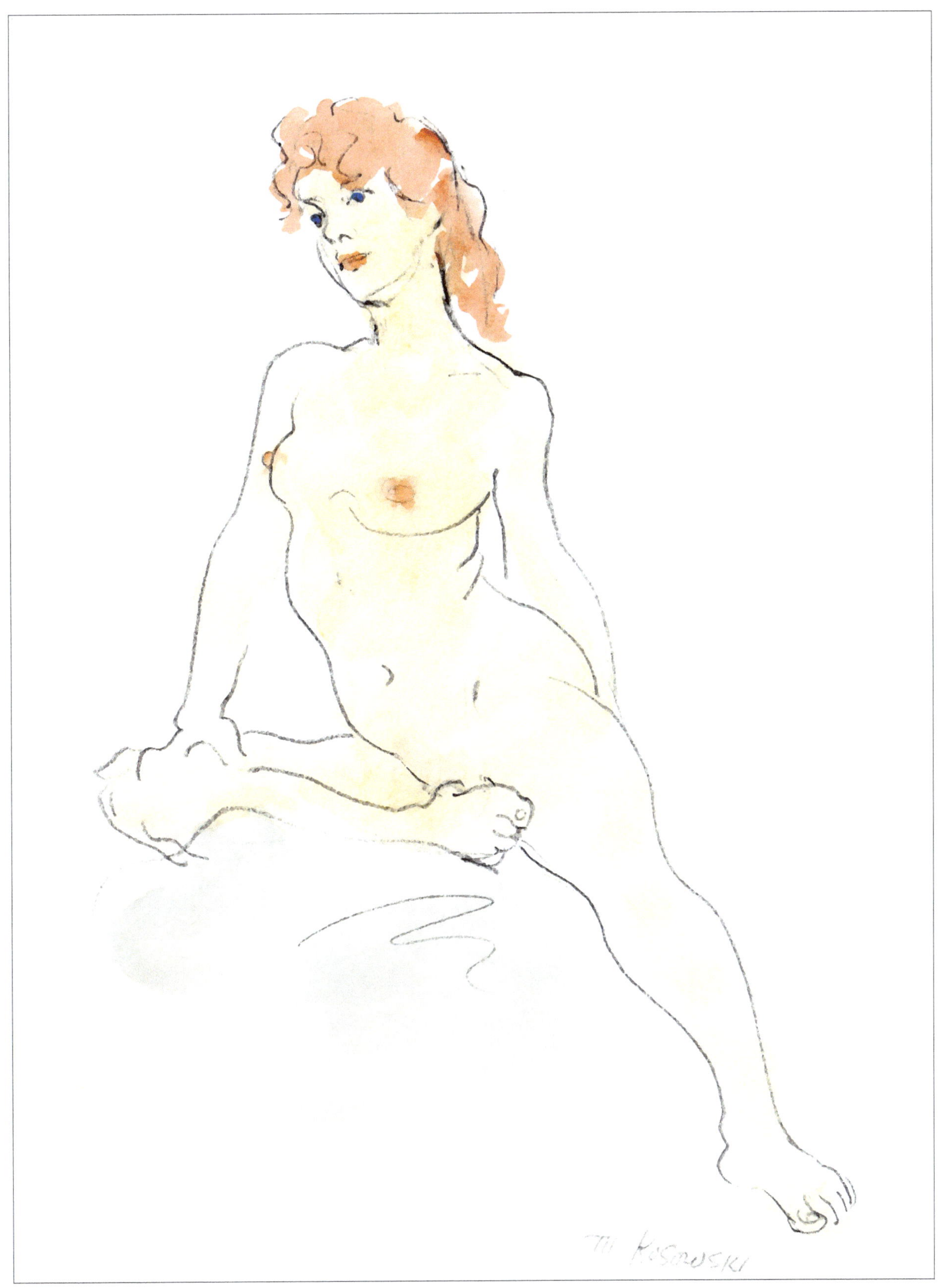

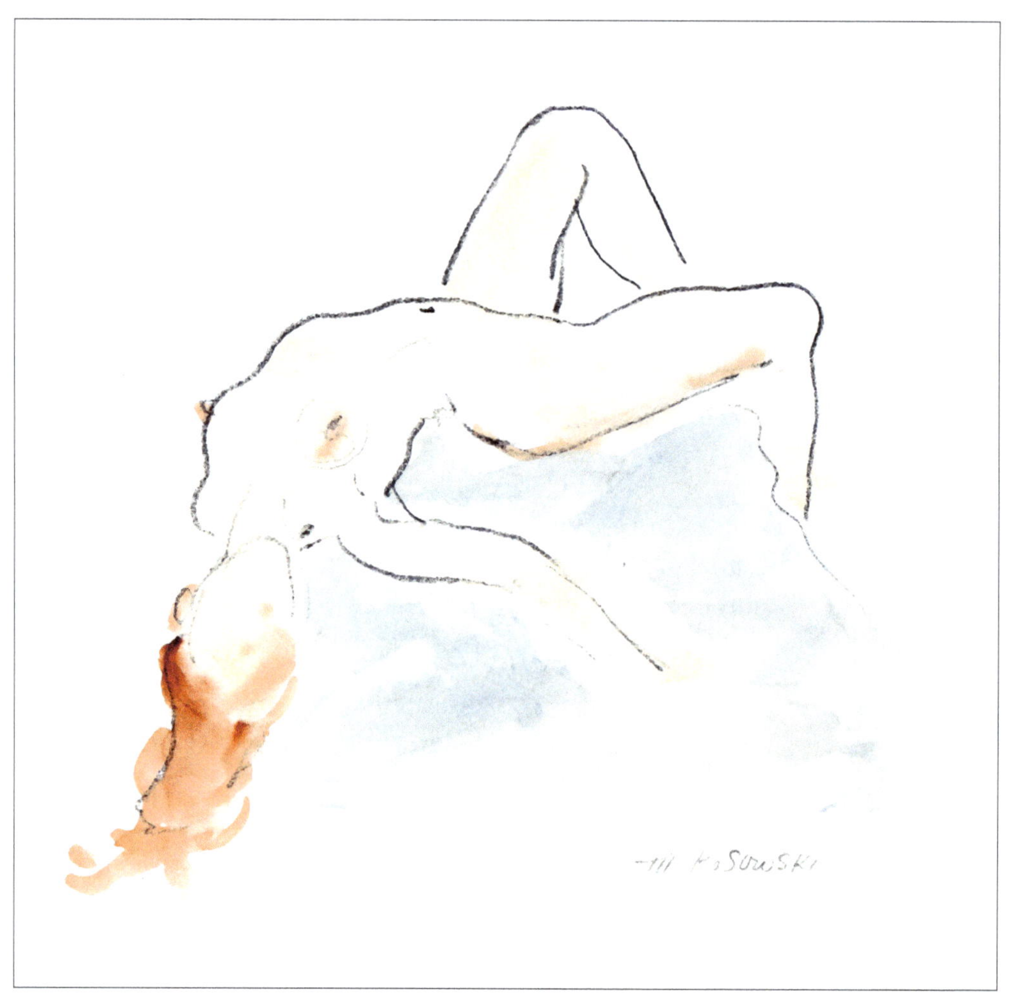

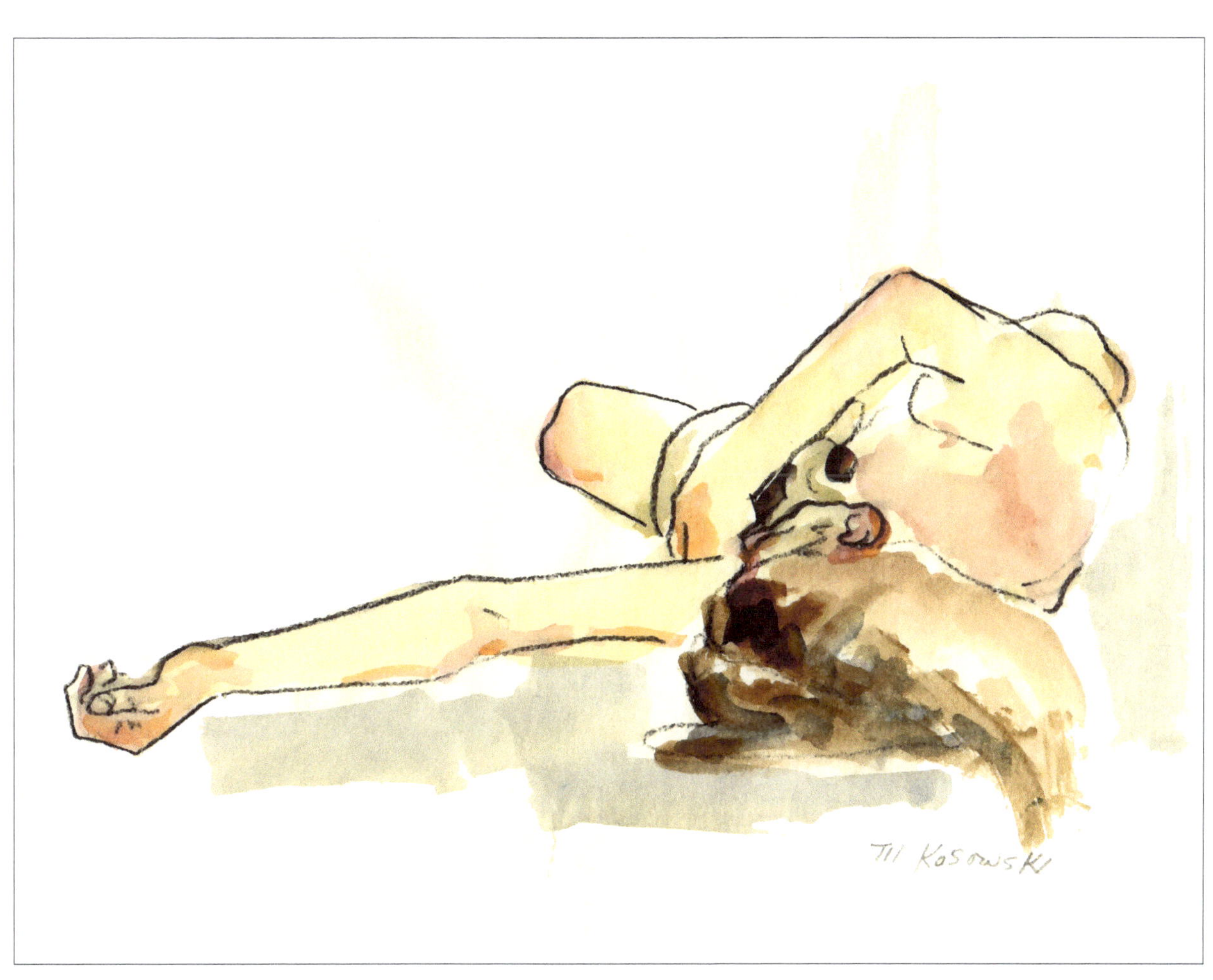

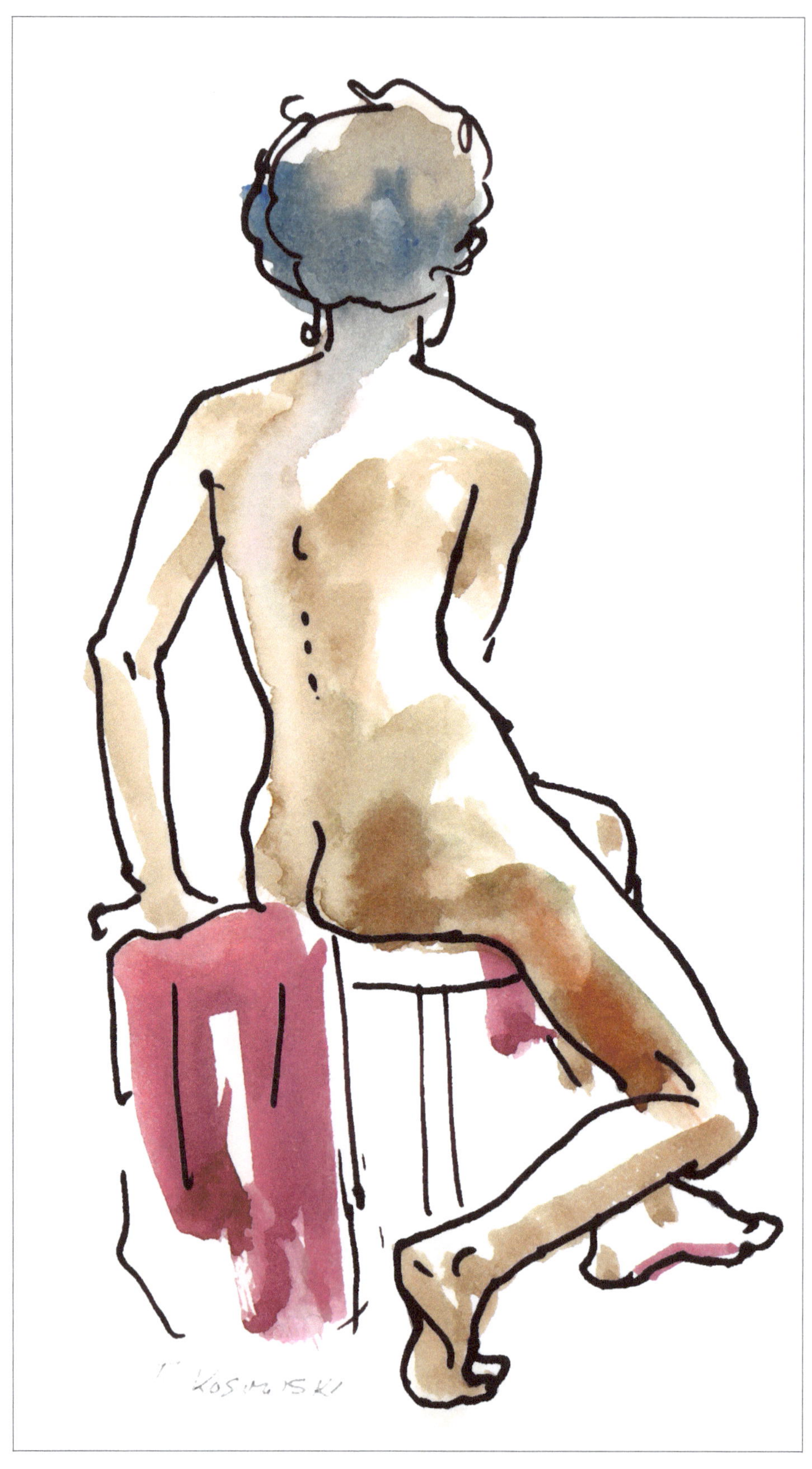

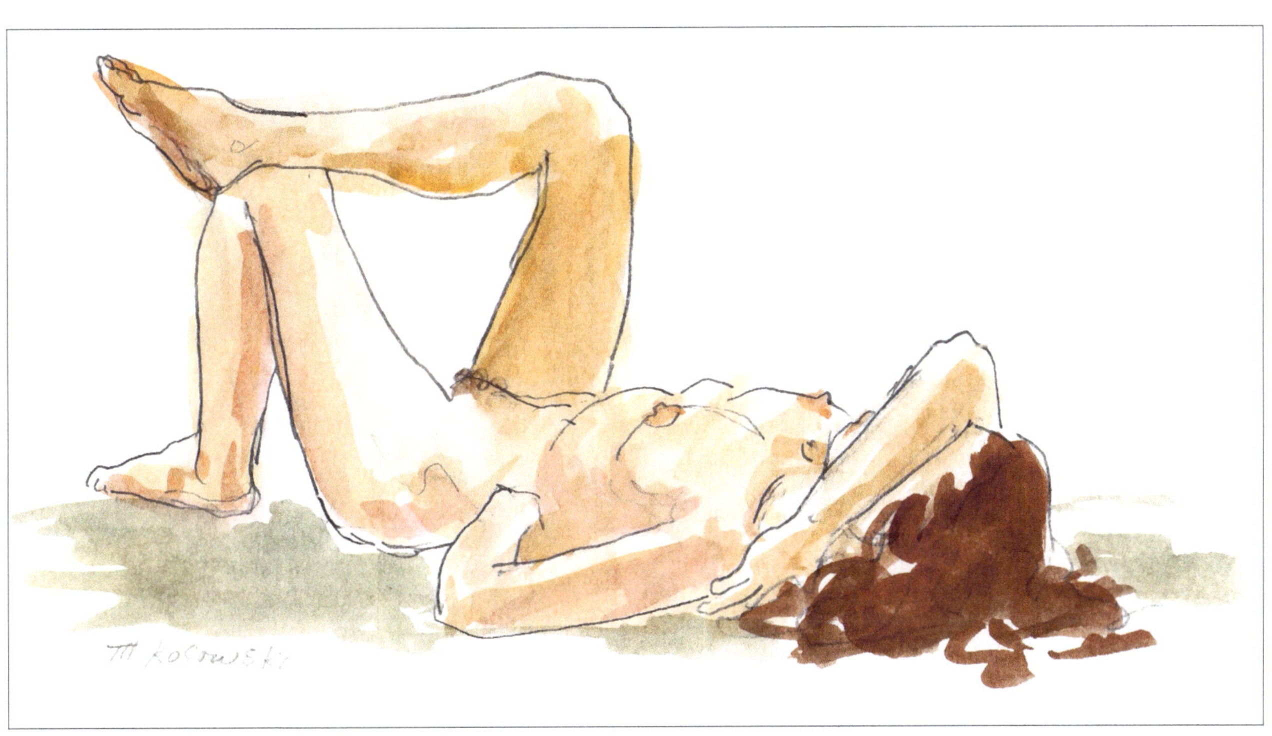

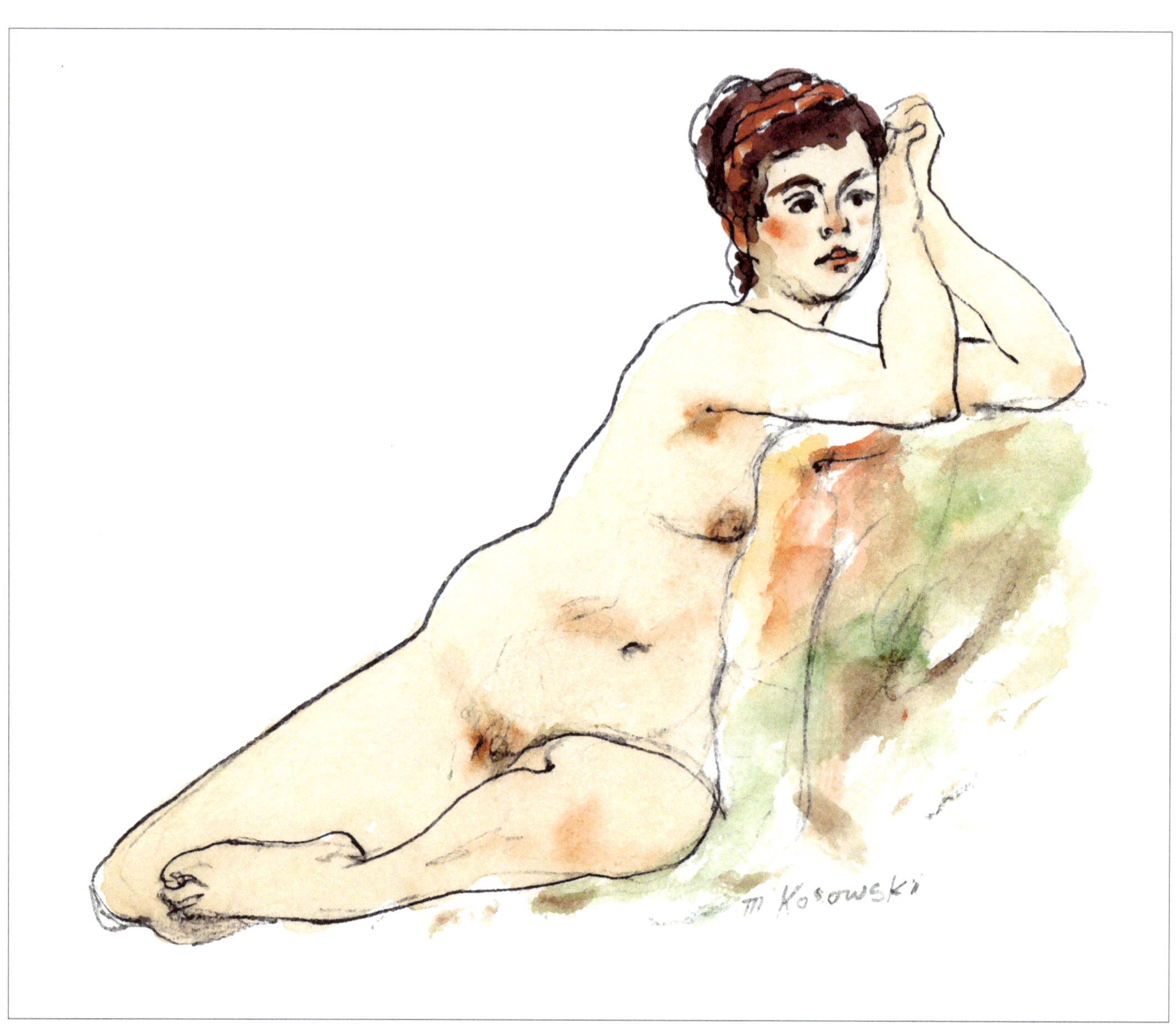
M Kosowski

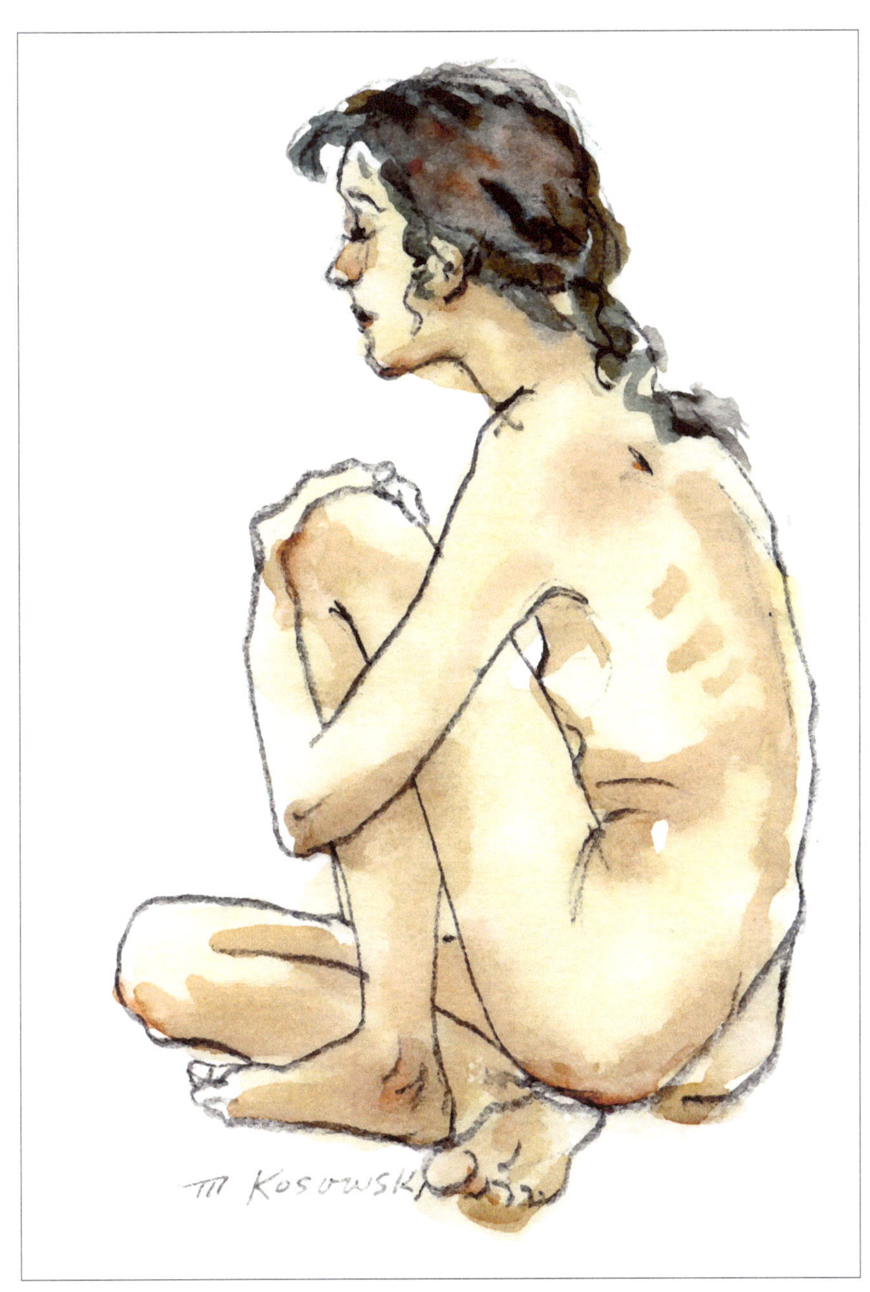
M Kosowski

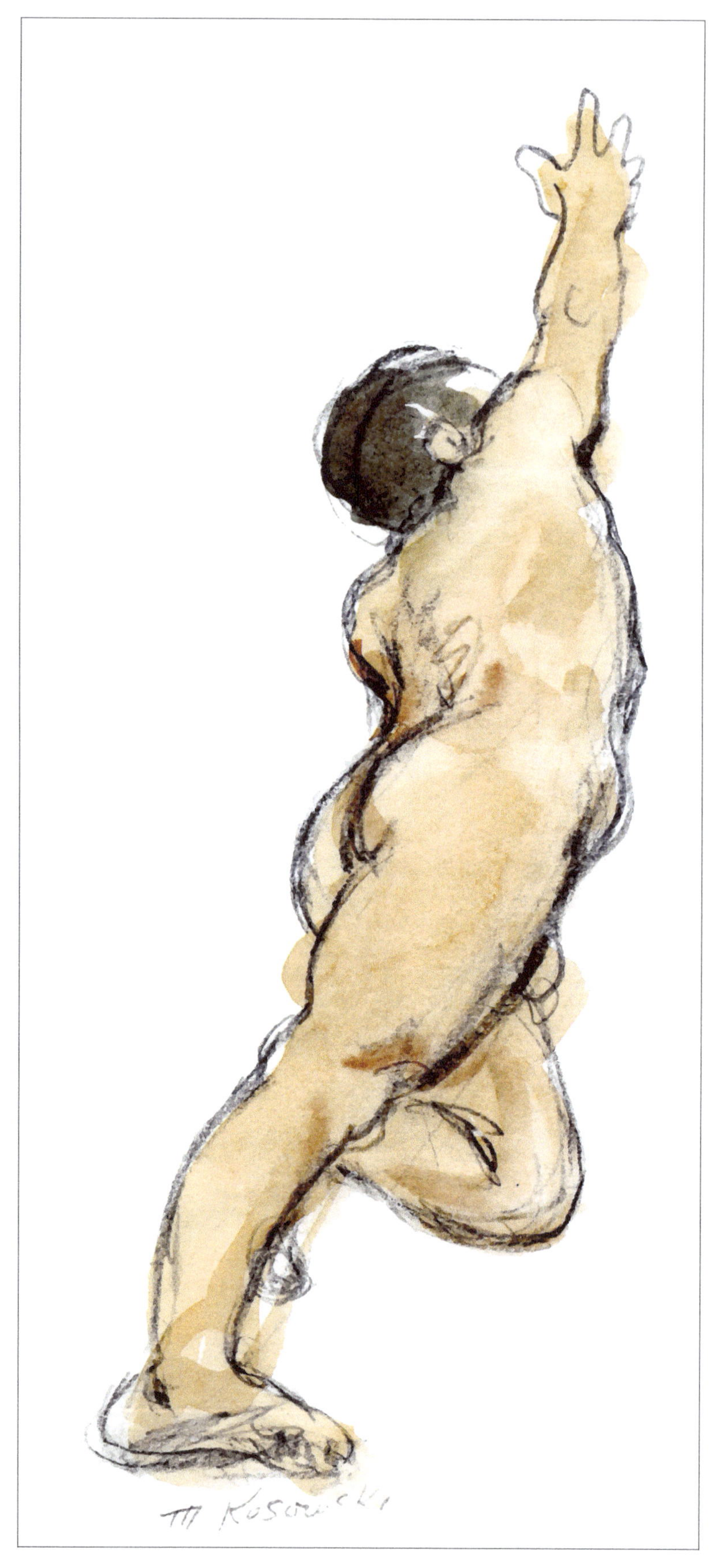

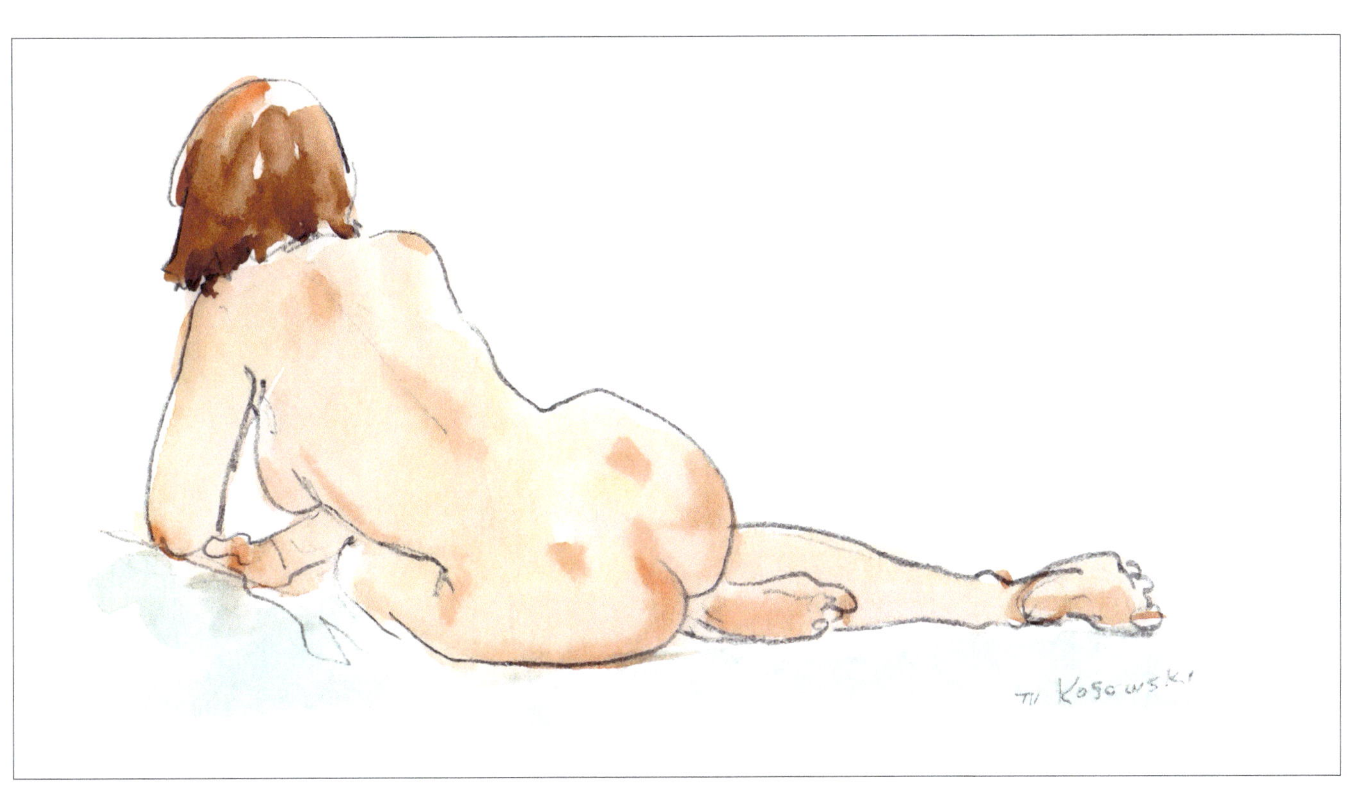
TH Kosowski

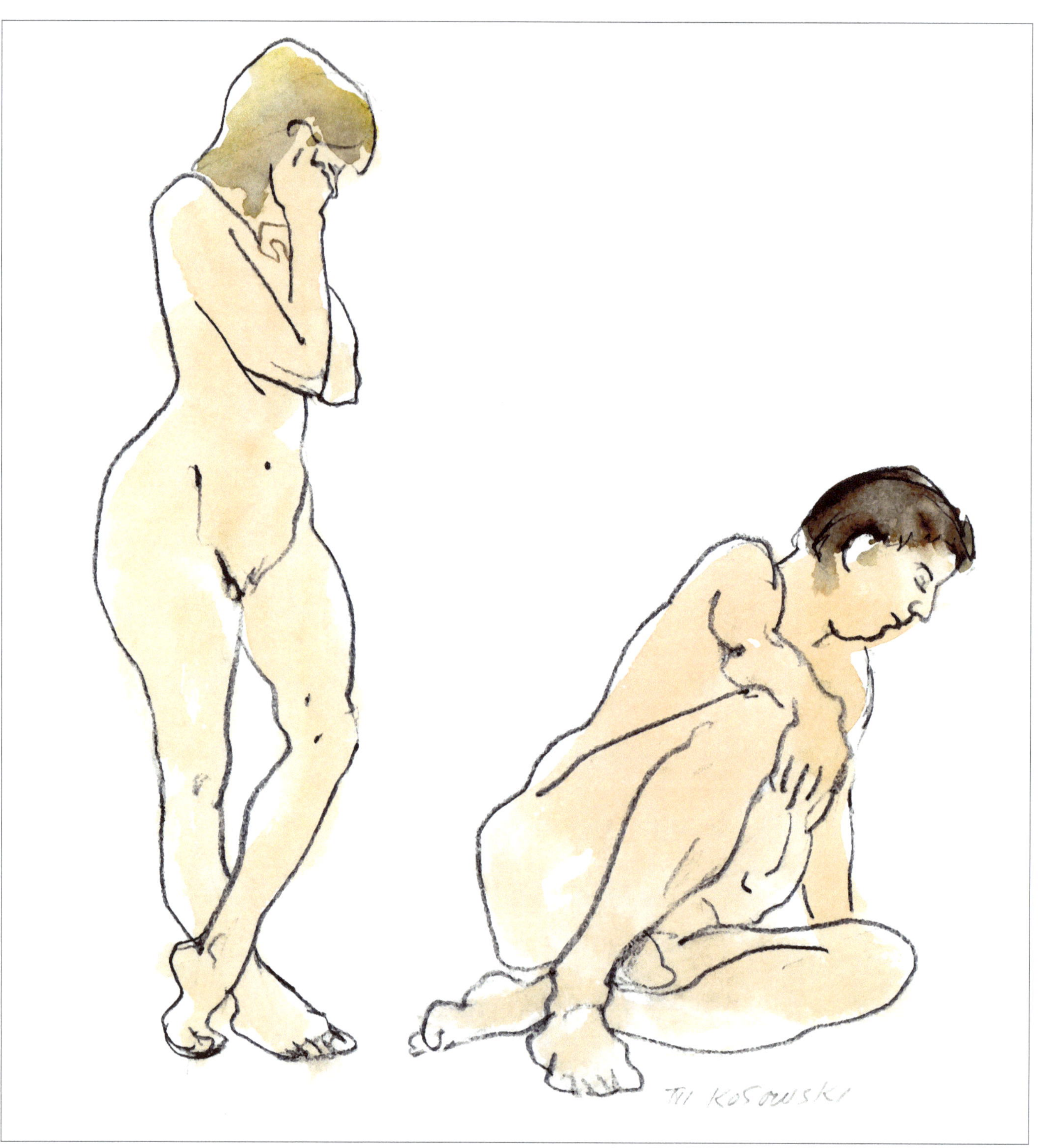
TM KOSOWSKI

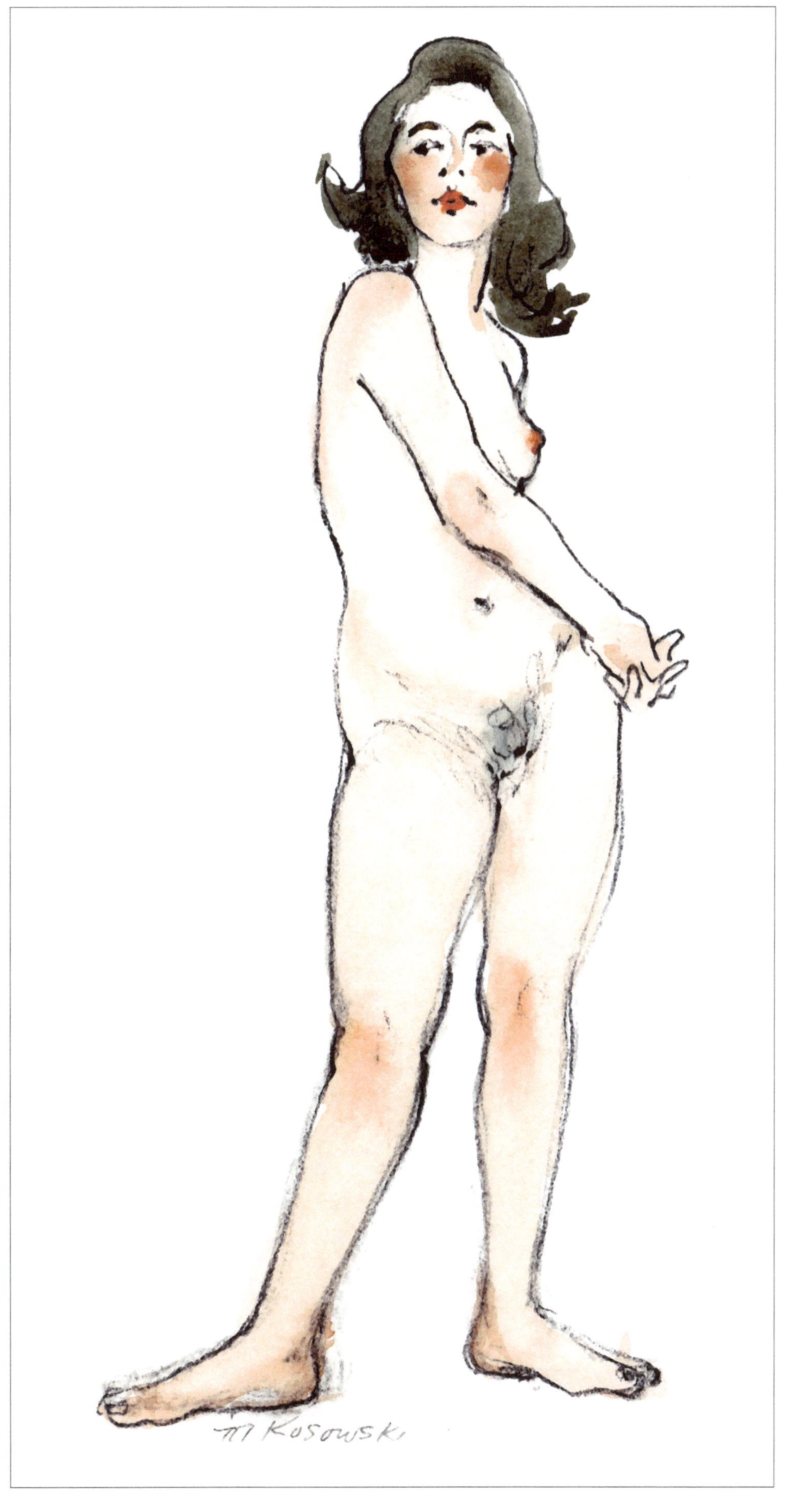
M Kosowski

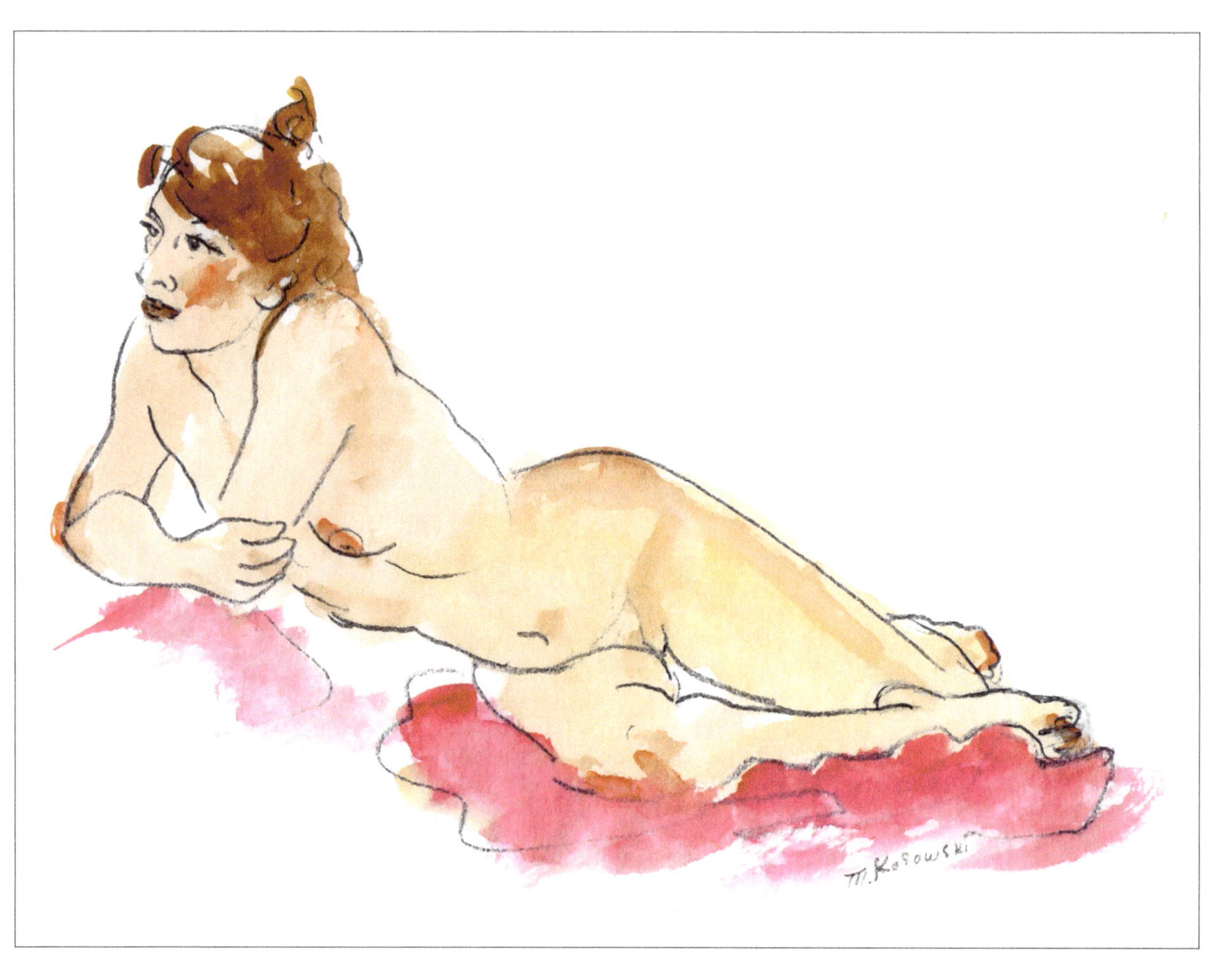
M. Kosowski

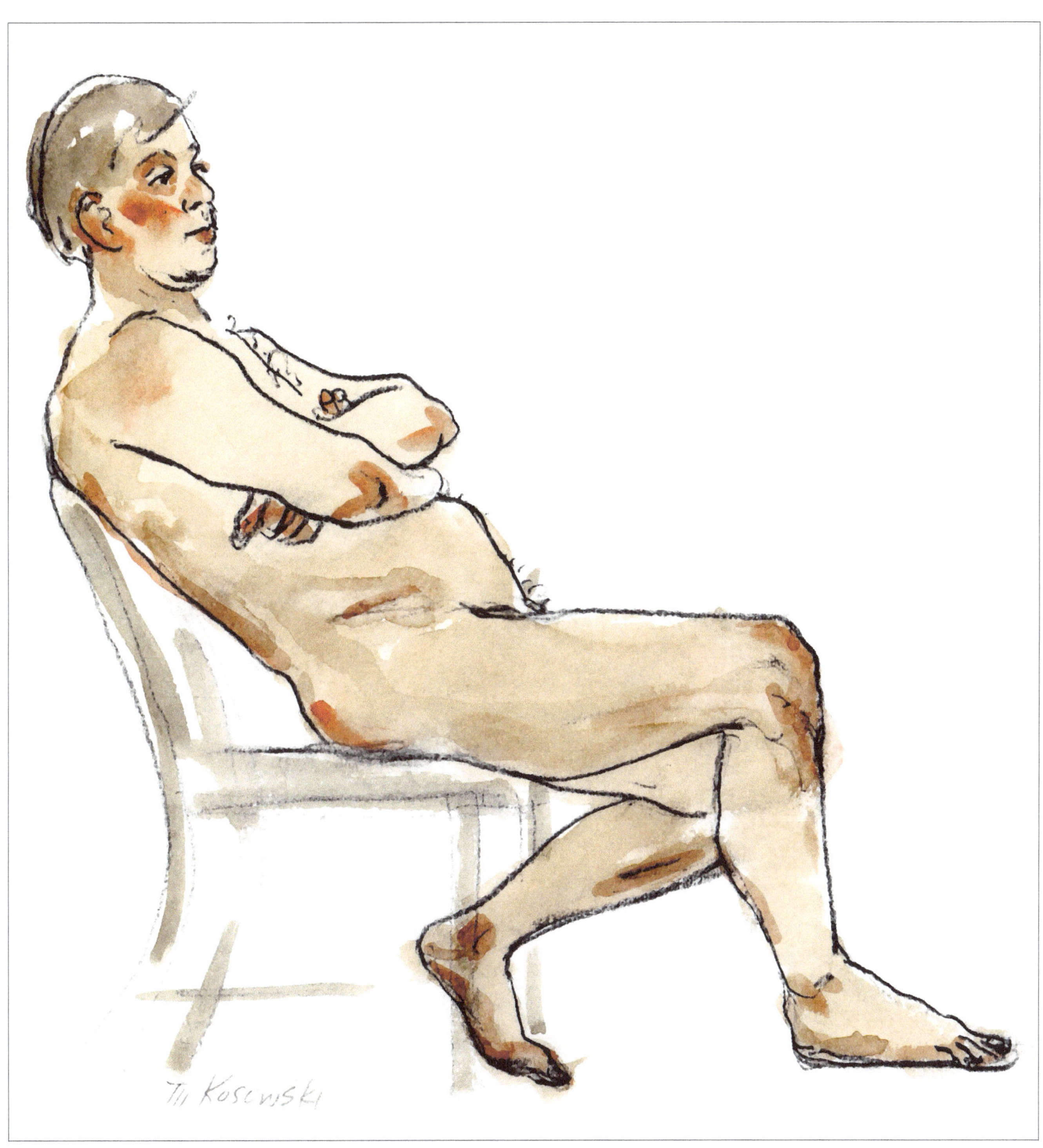

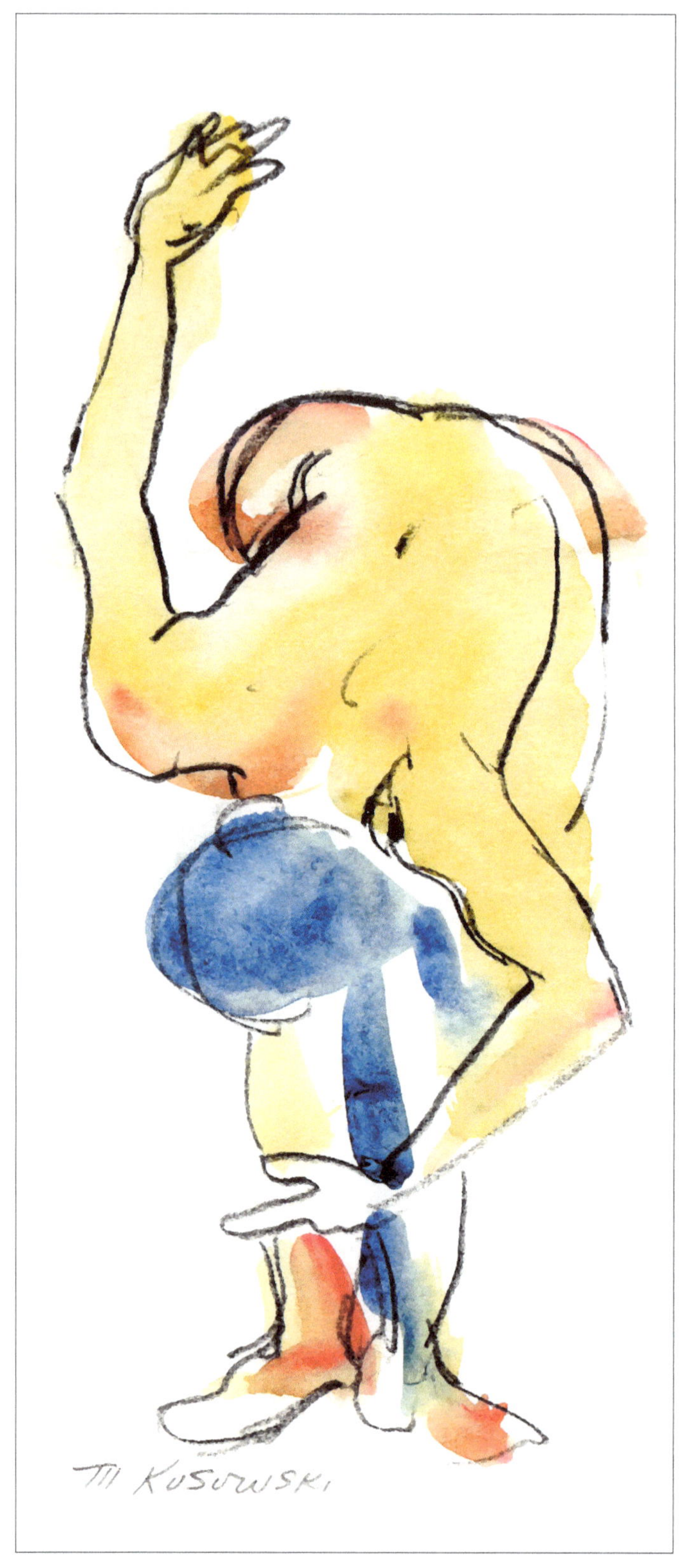

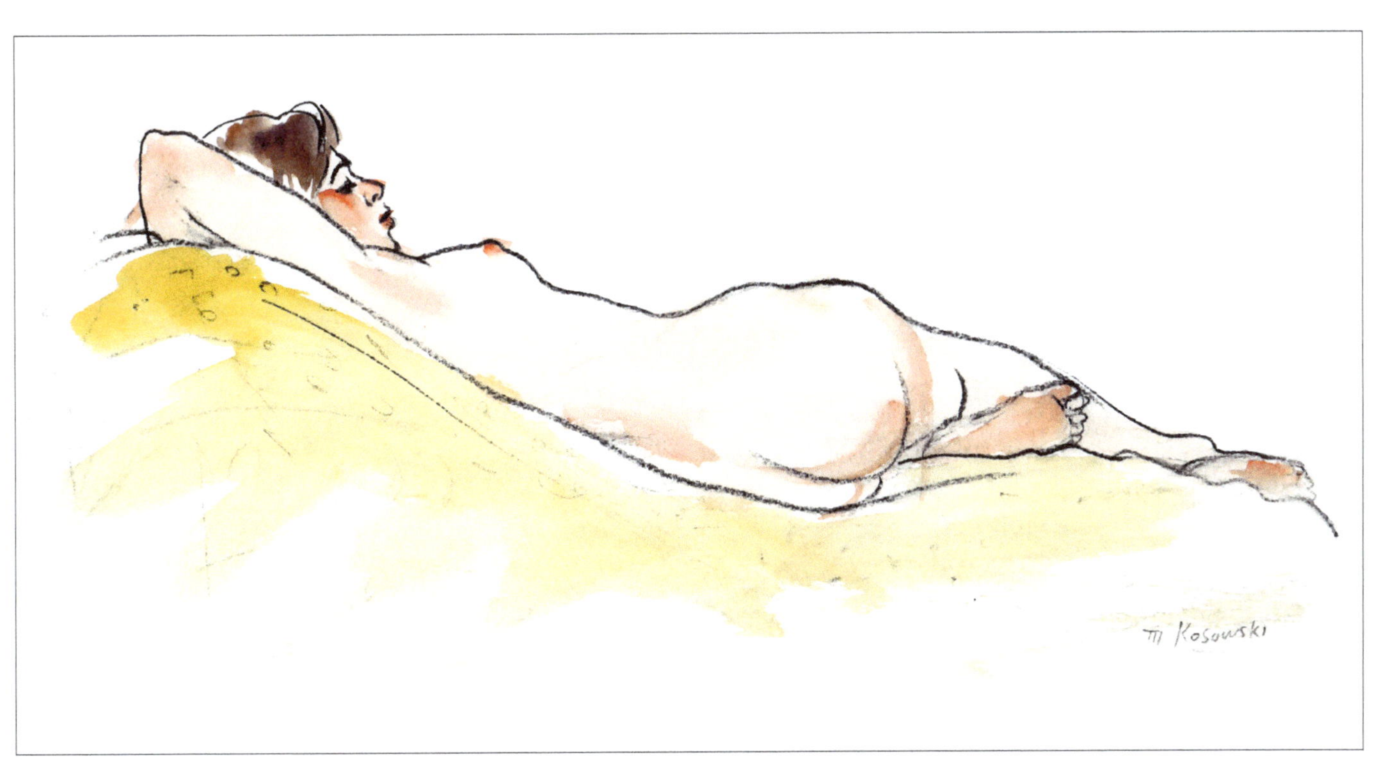
M Kosowski

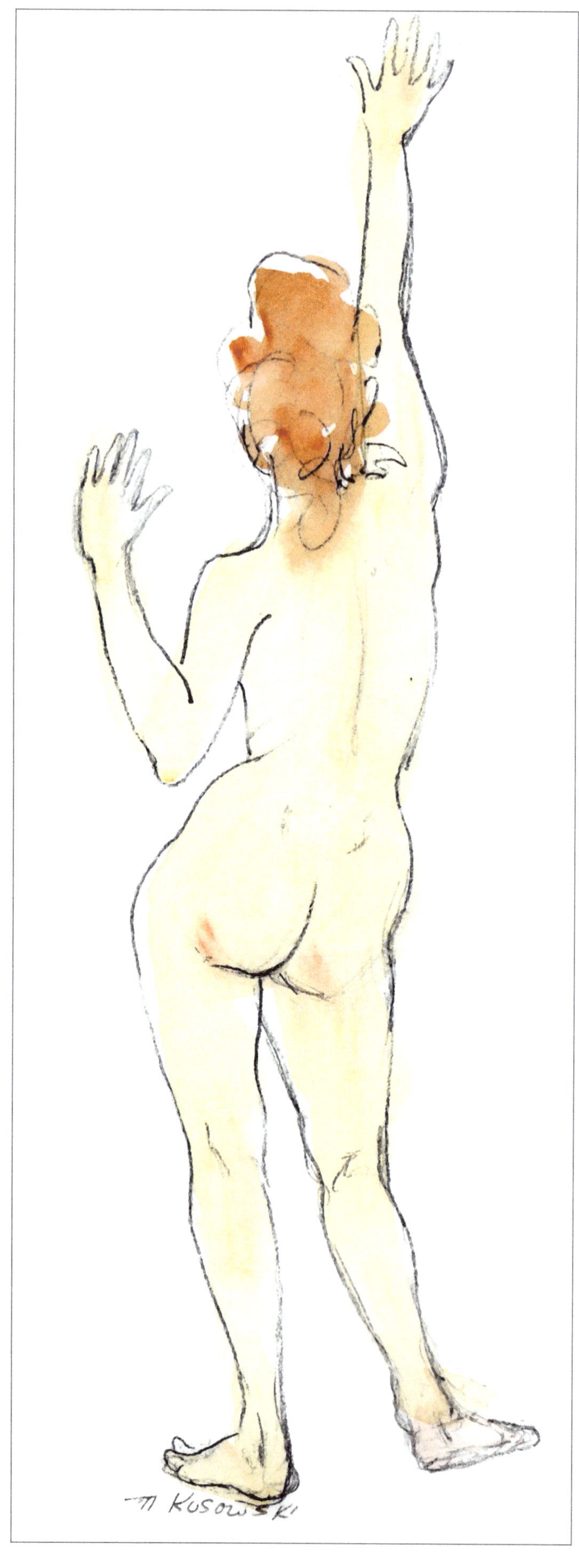

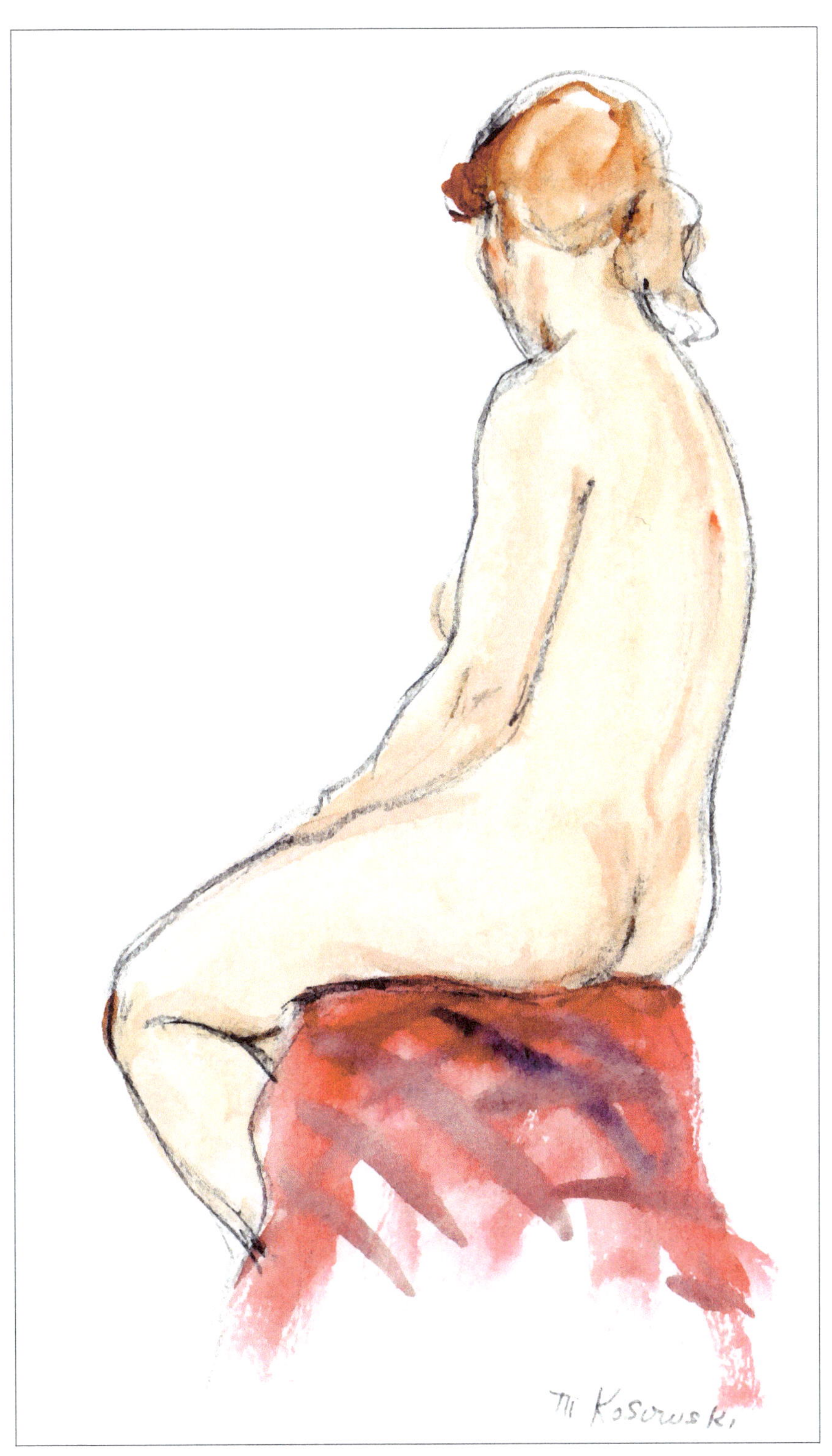
M Kosowski

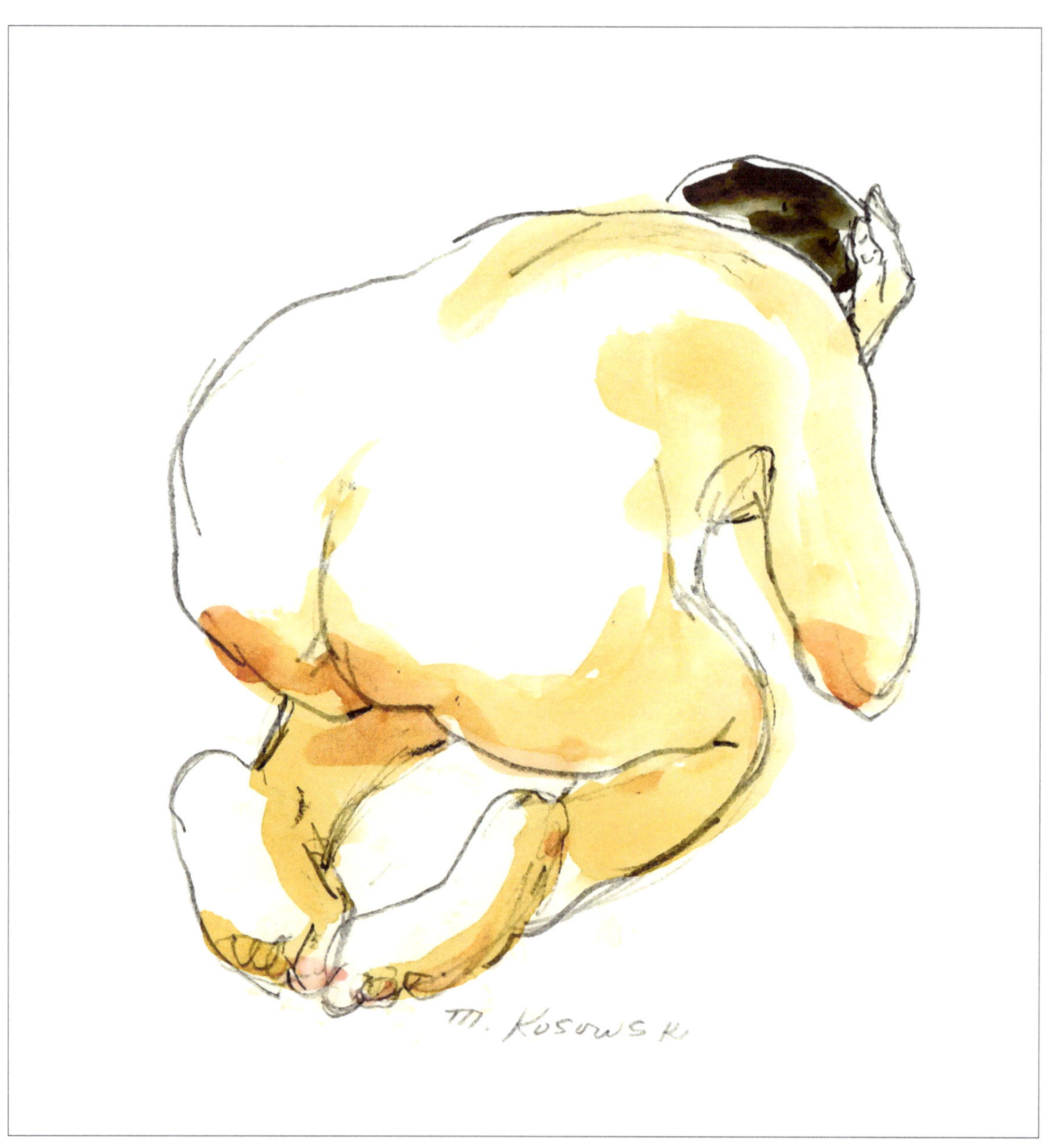
M. Kosowski

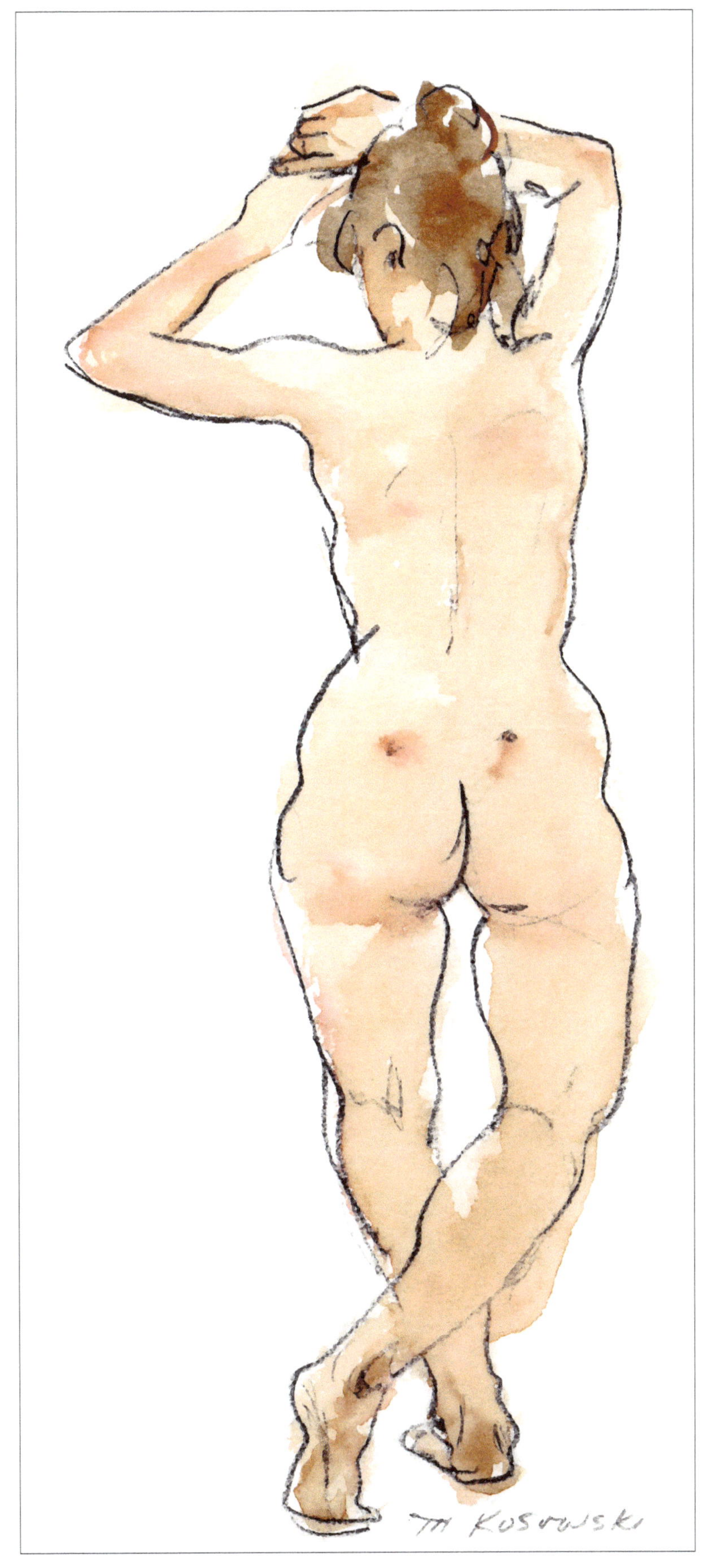
M KOSOWSKI

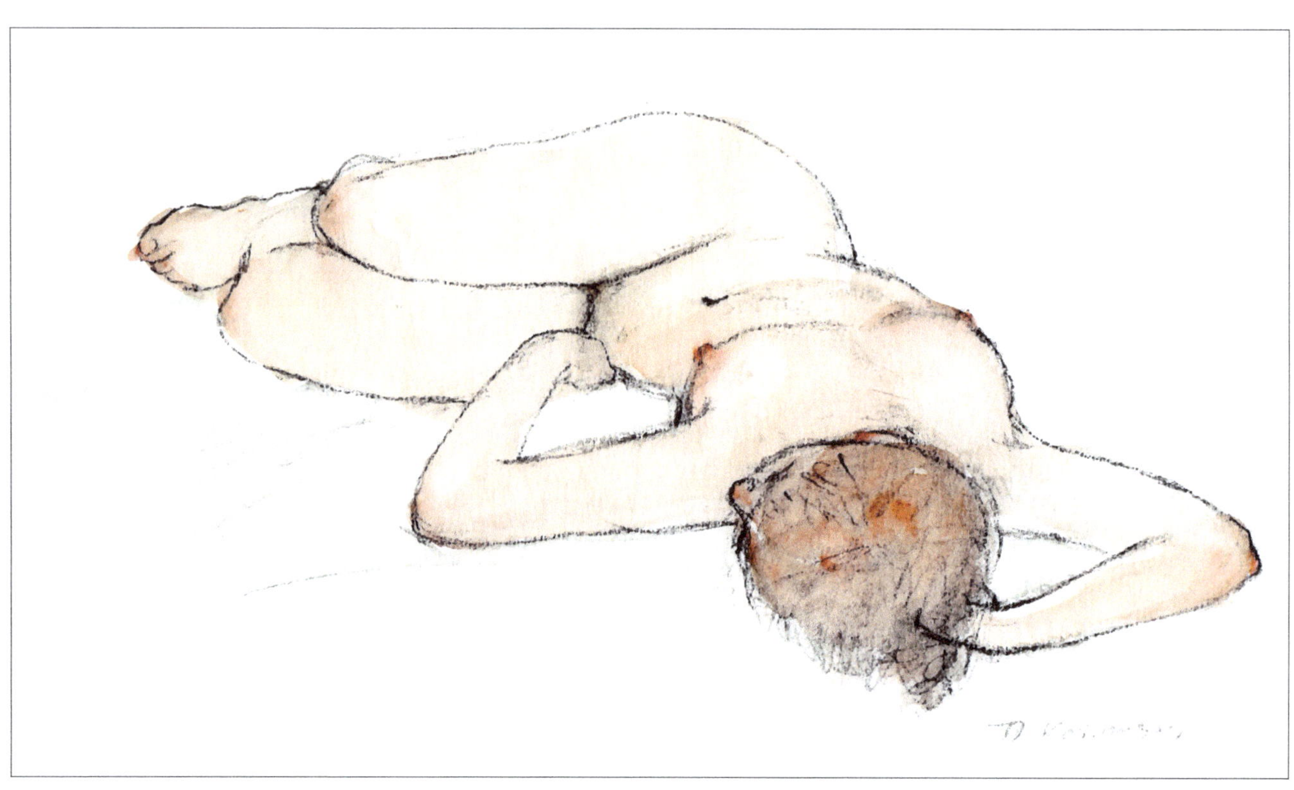

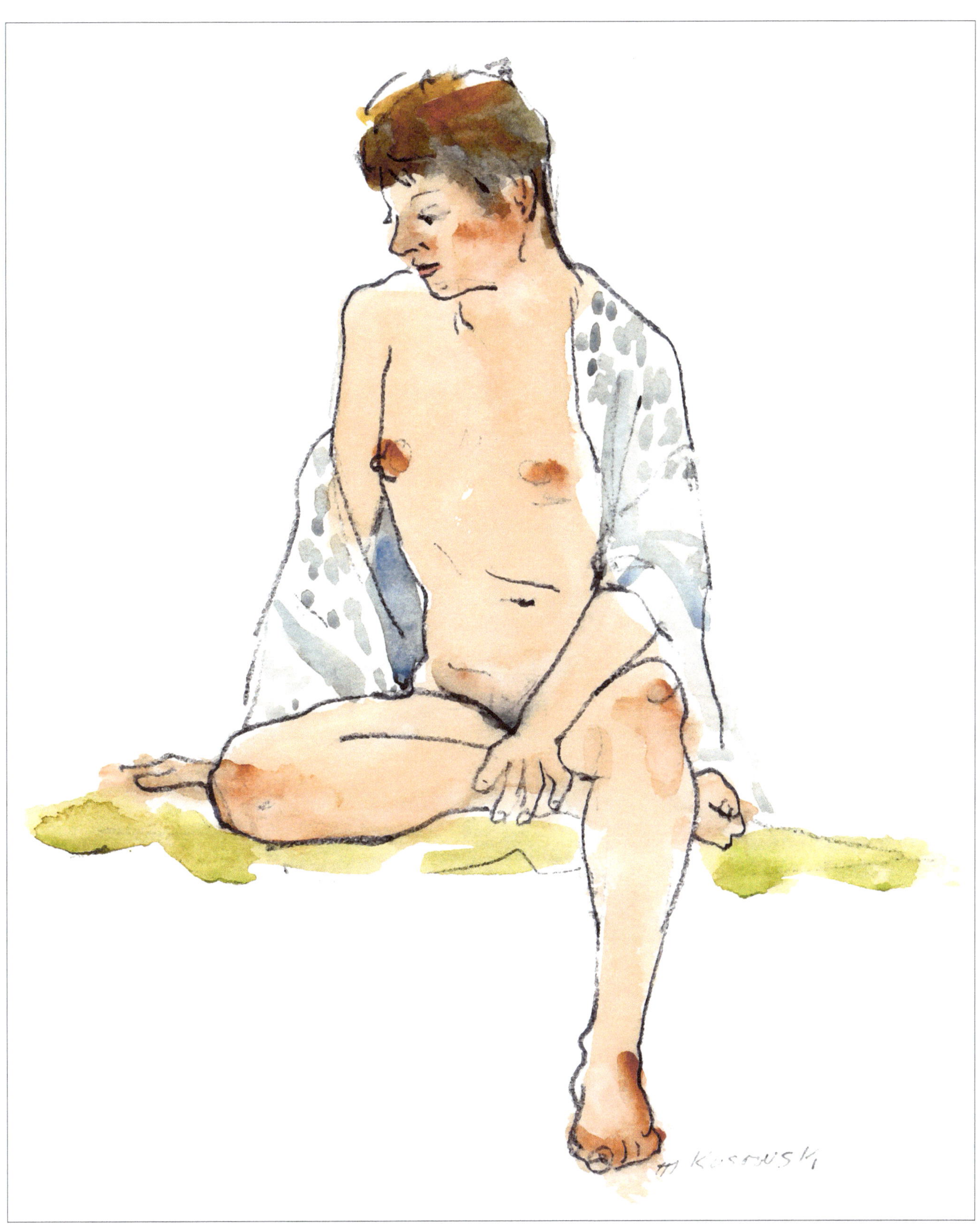

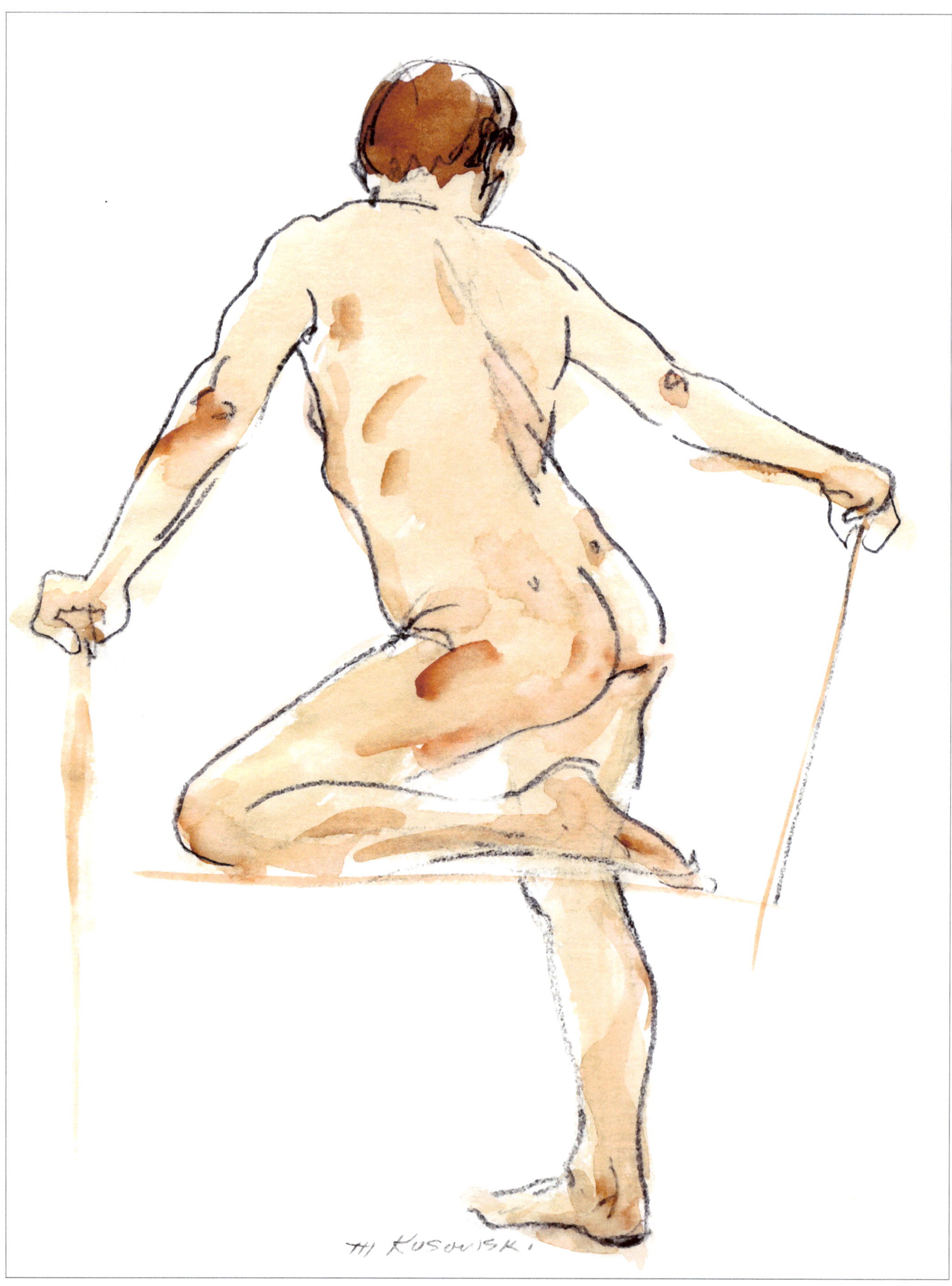

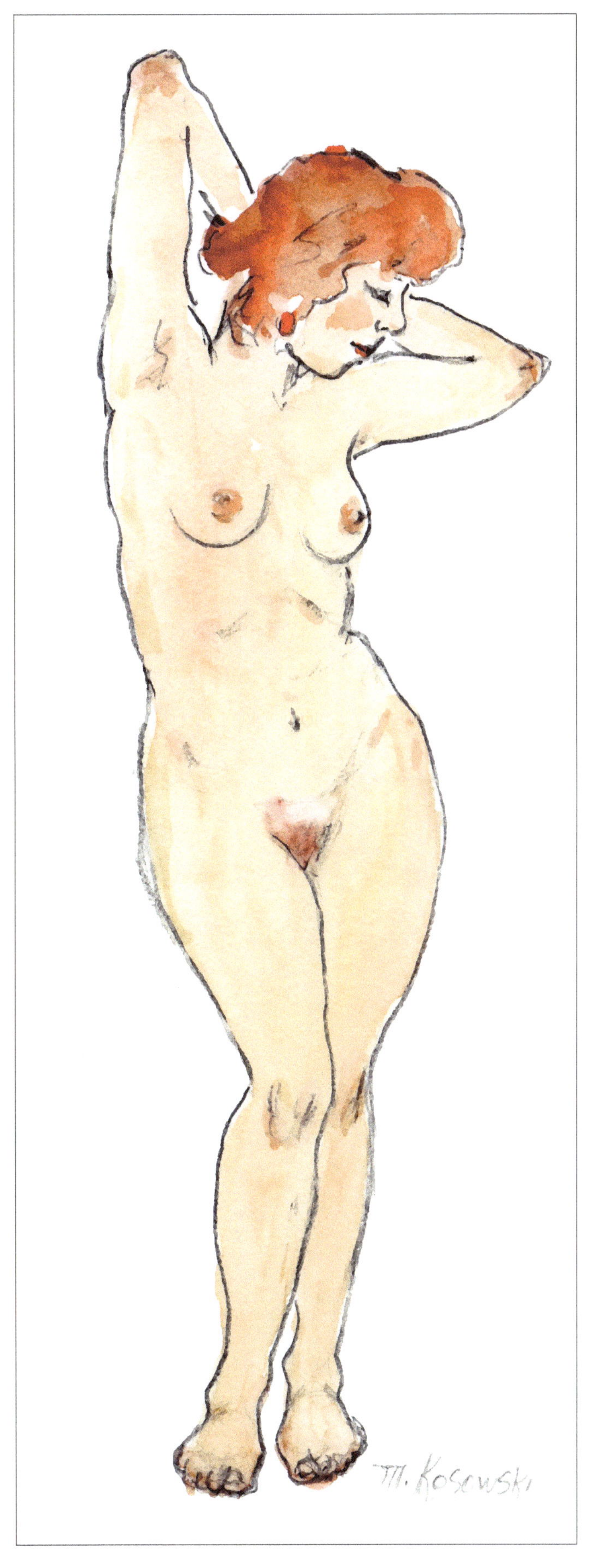
M. Kosewski

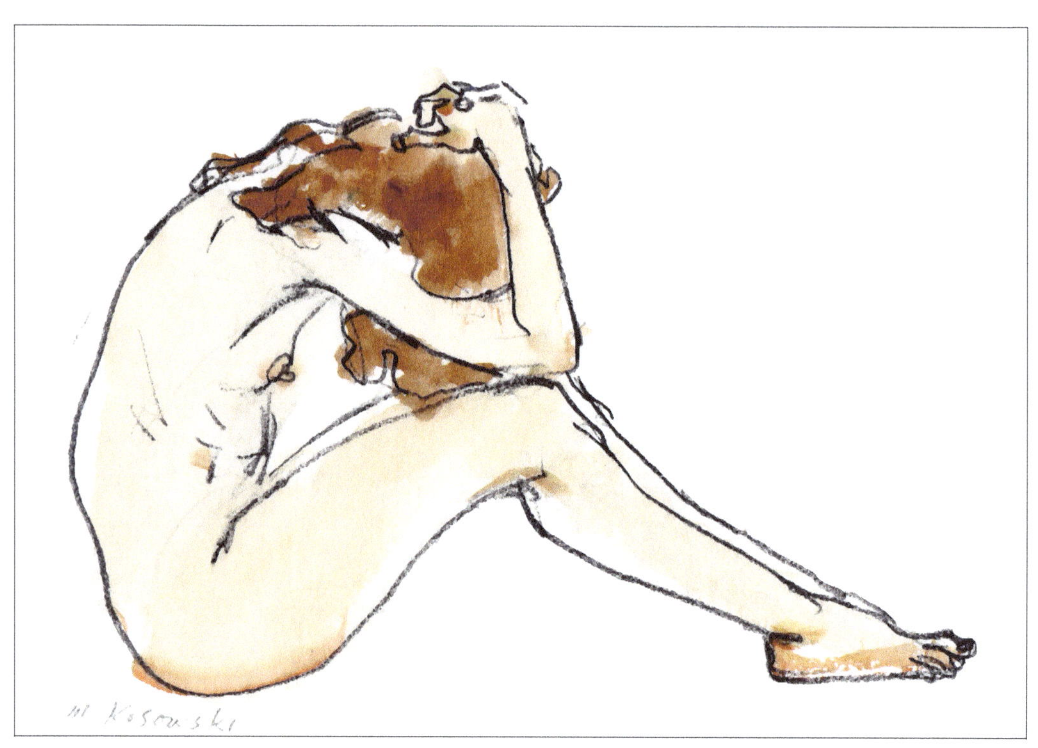

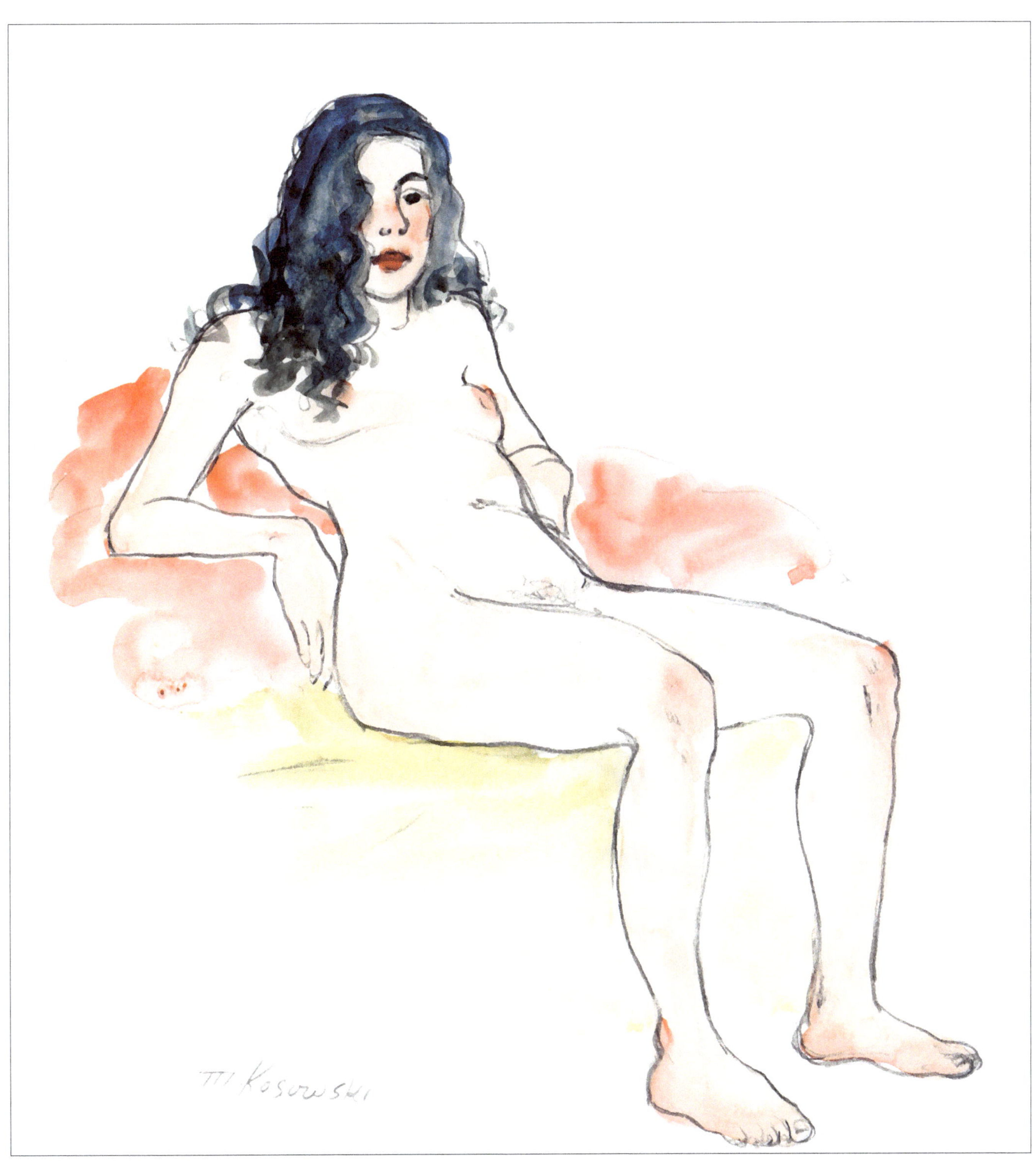
M Kosowski

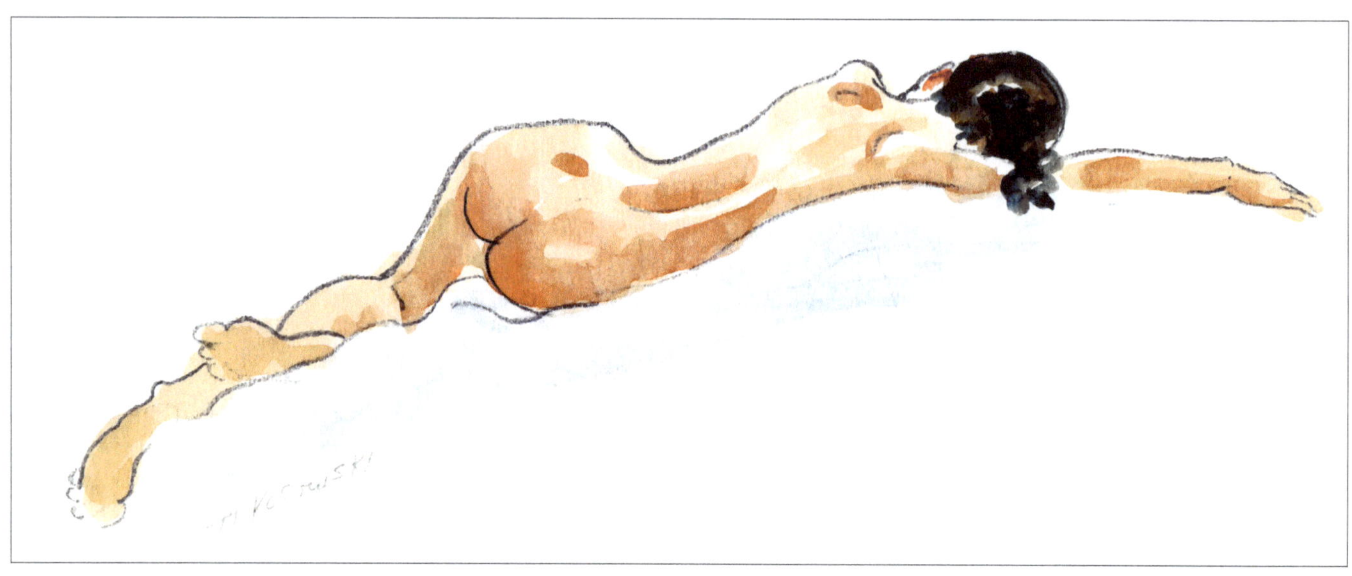

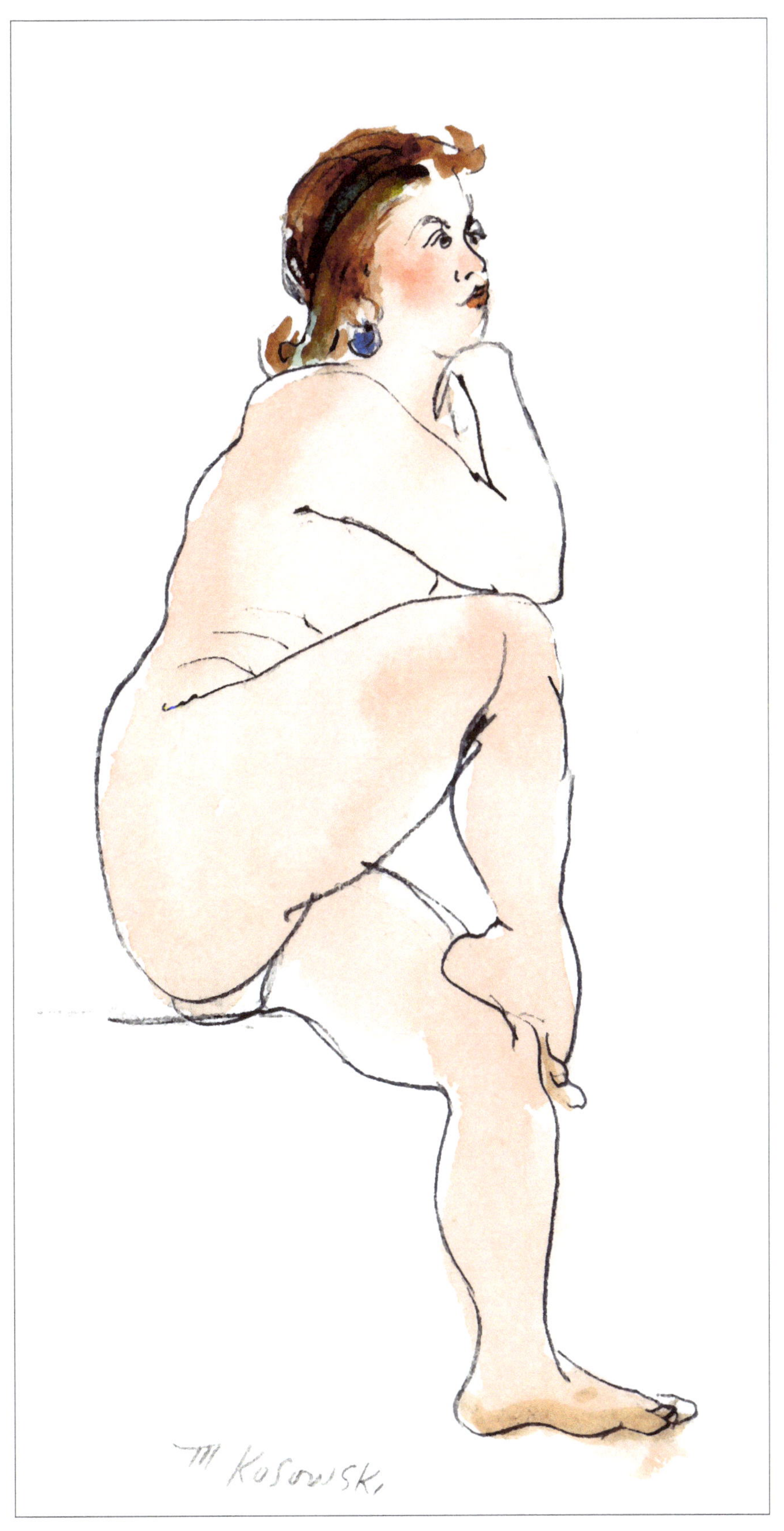
M Kosowski

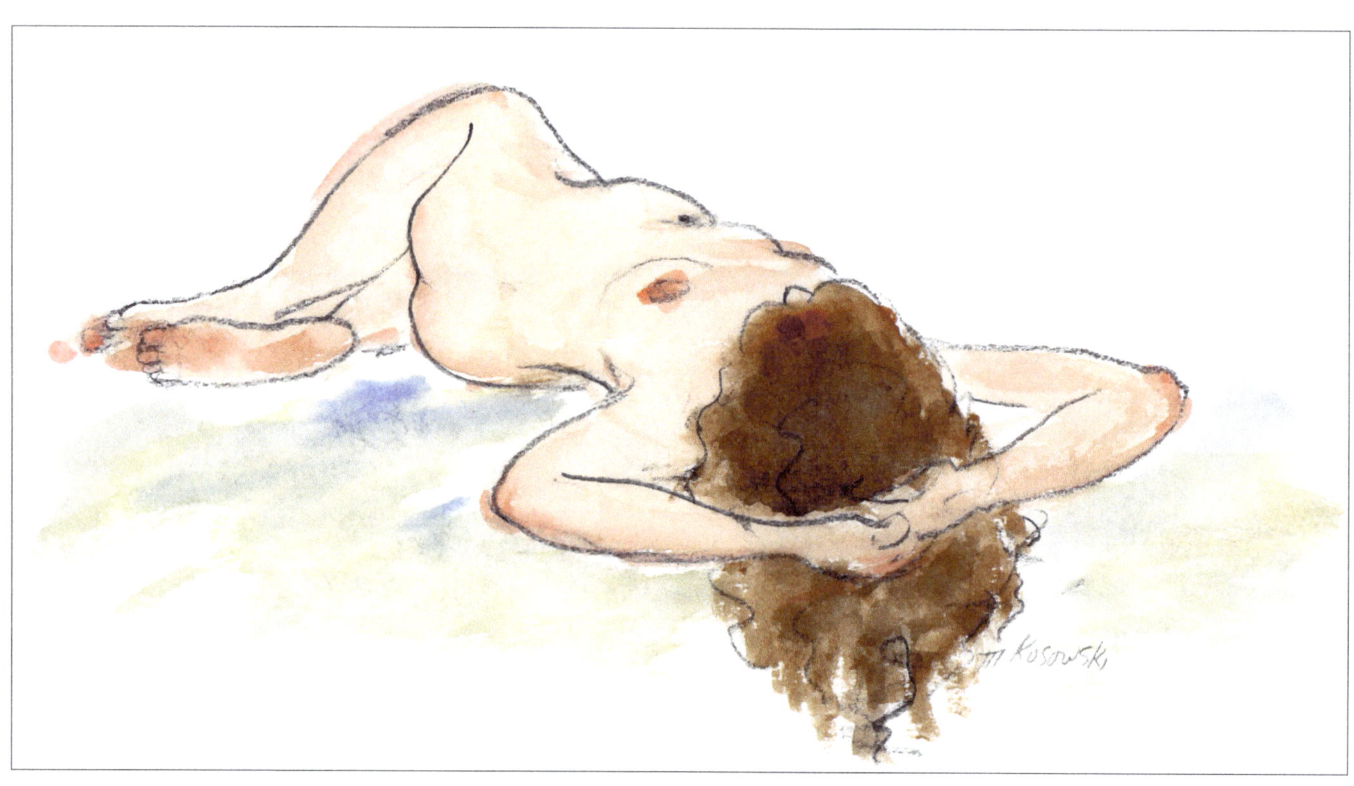

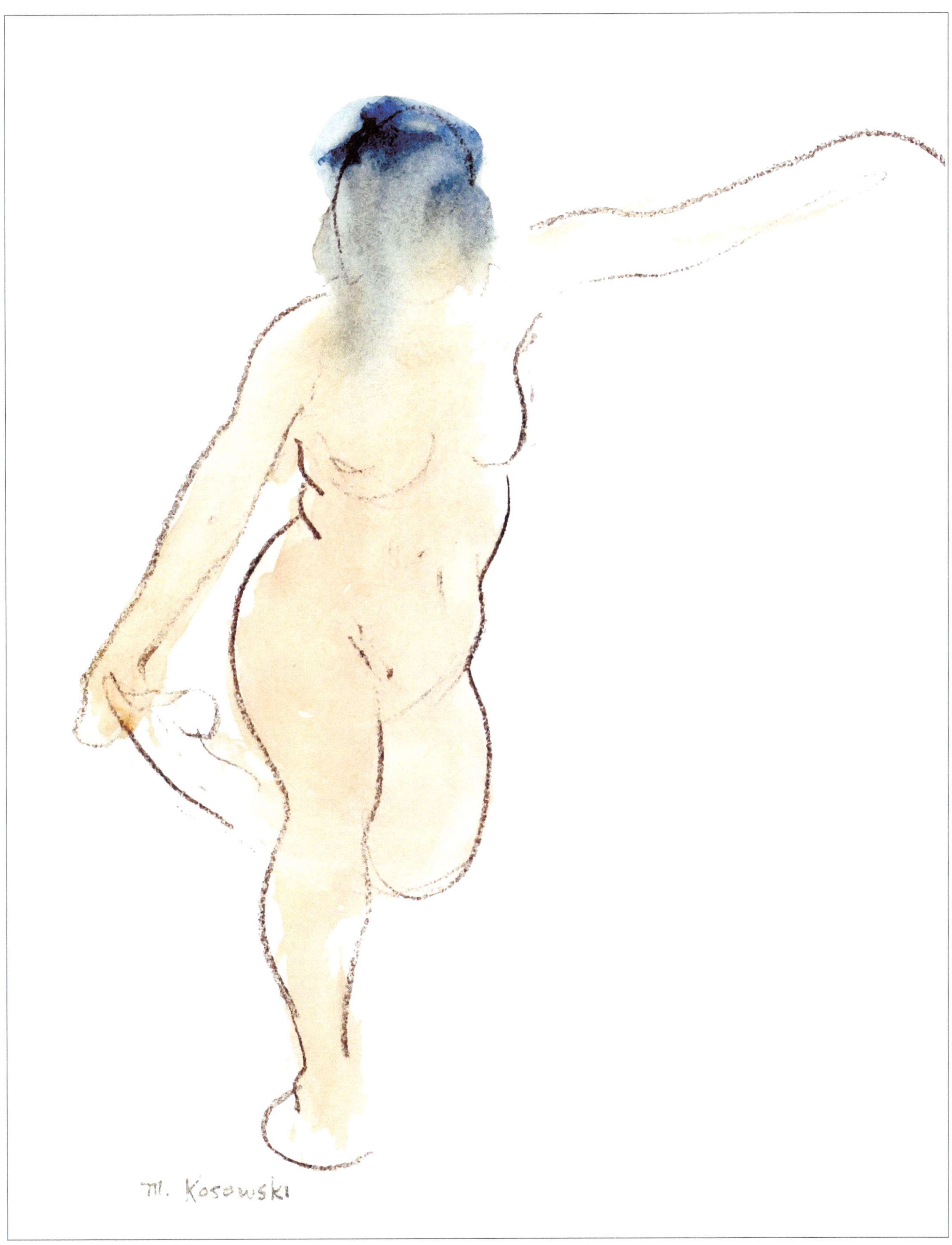
M. Kosowski

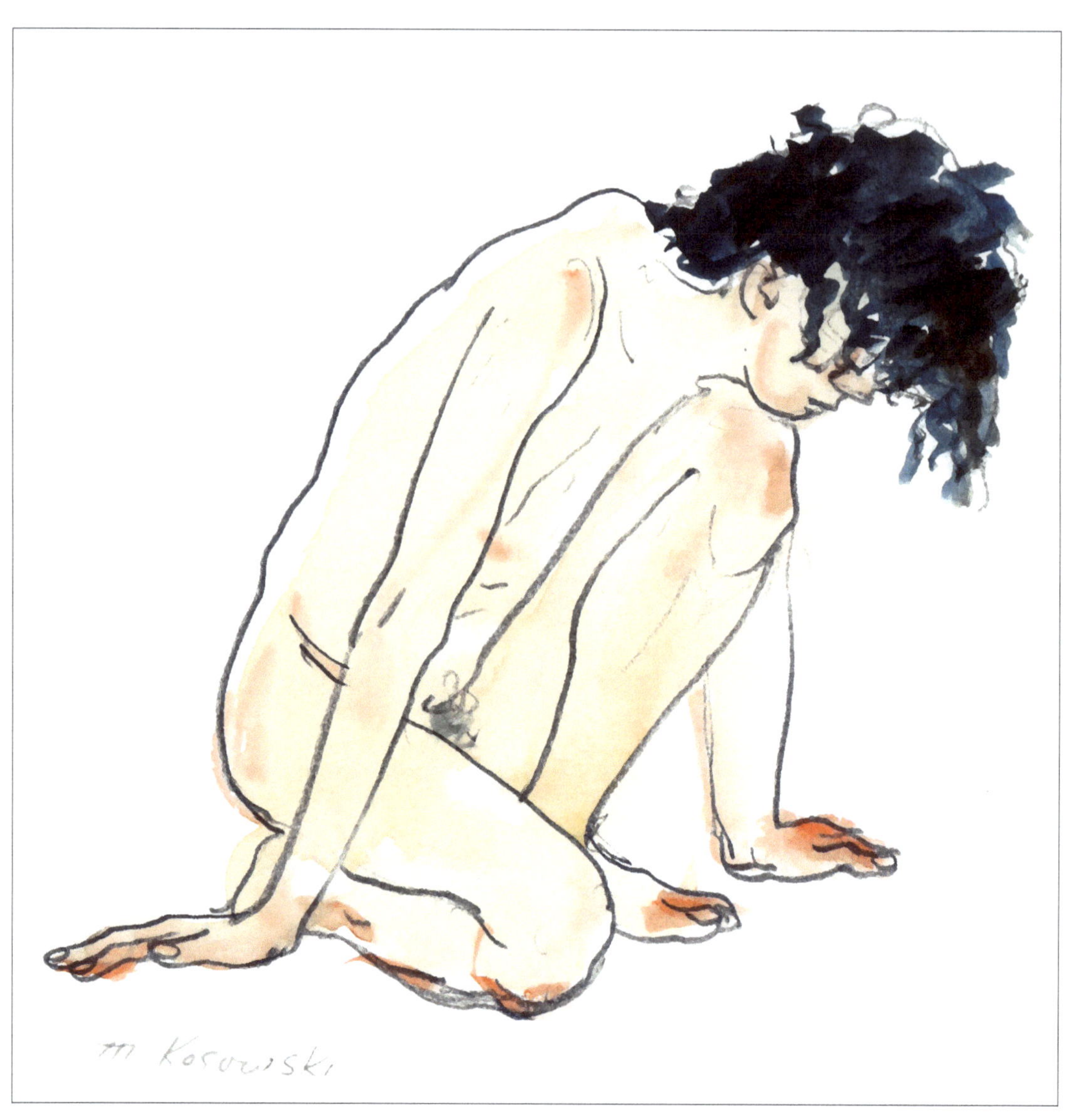
m Kosowski

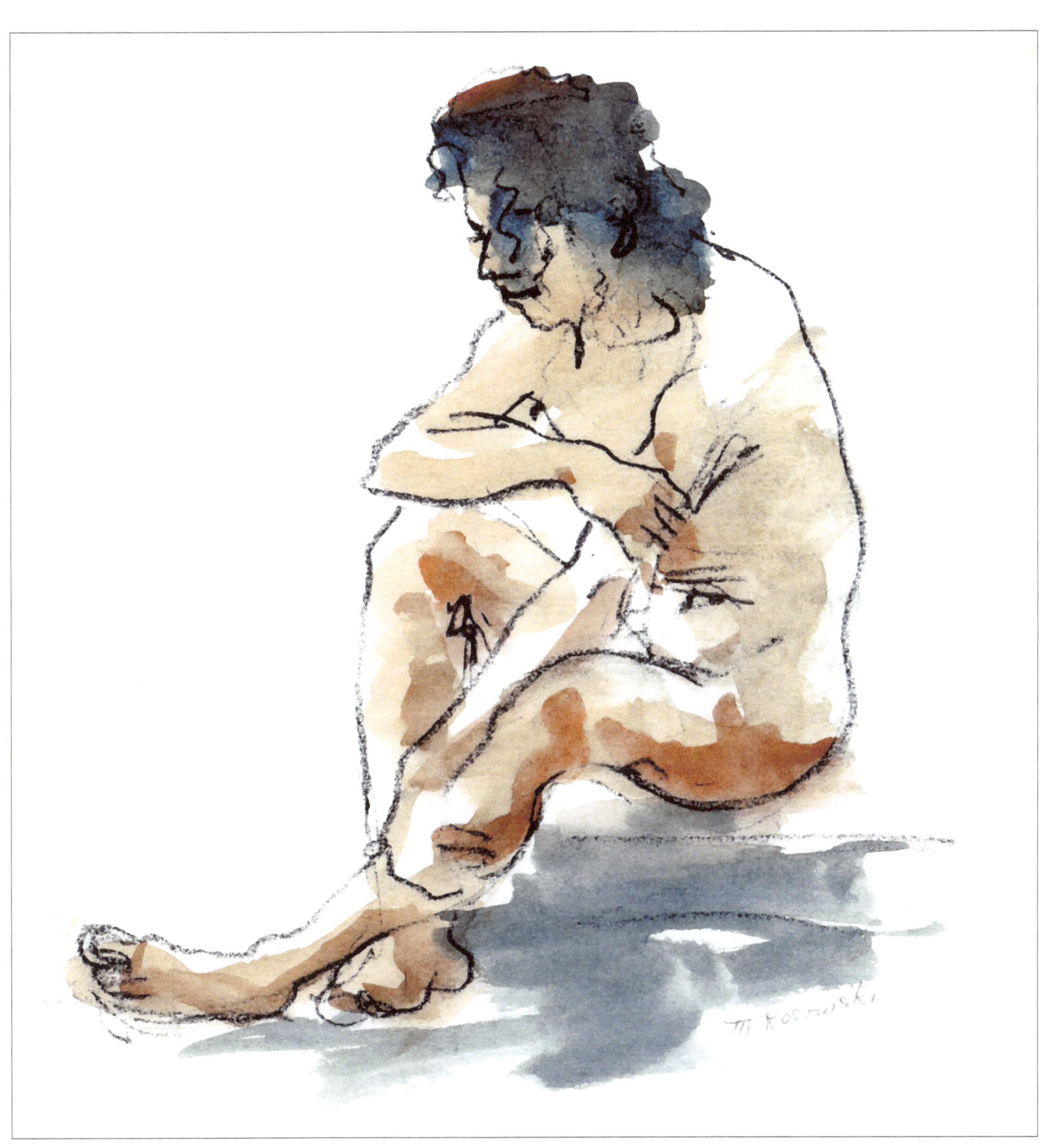

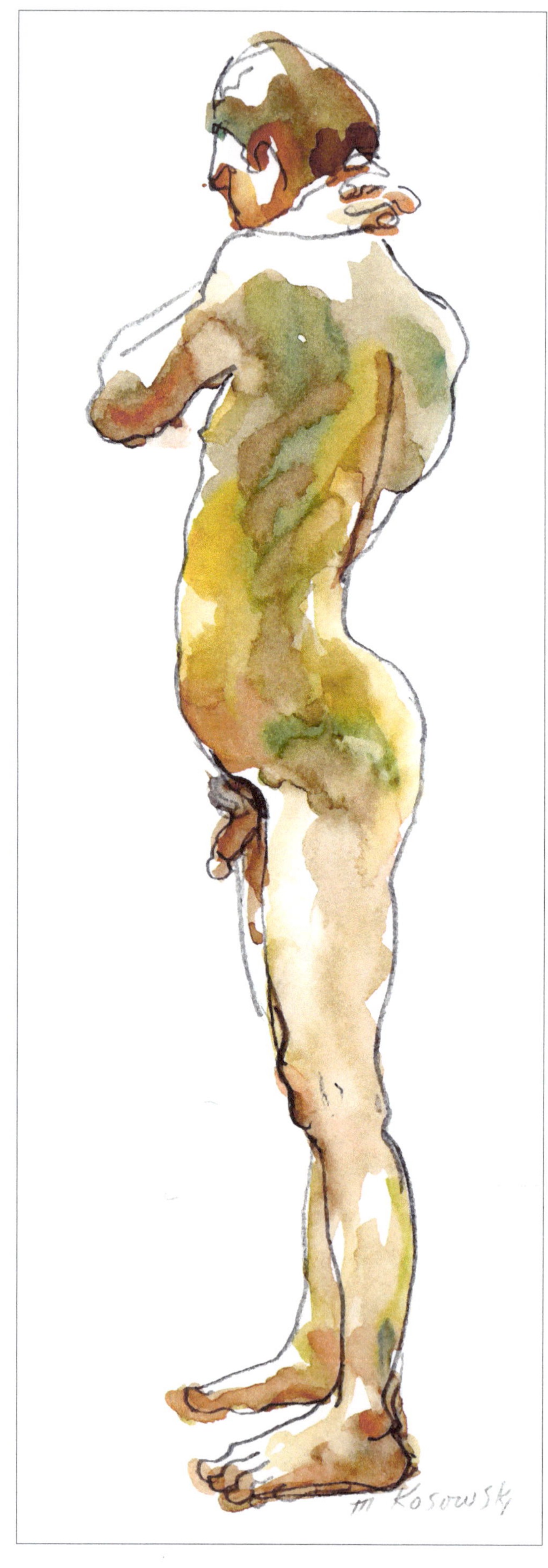
m Kosowsky

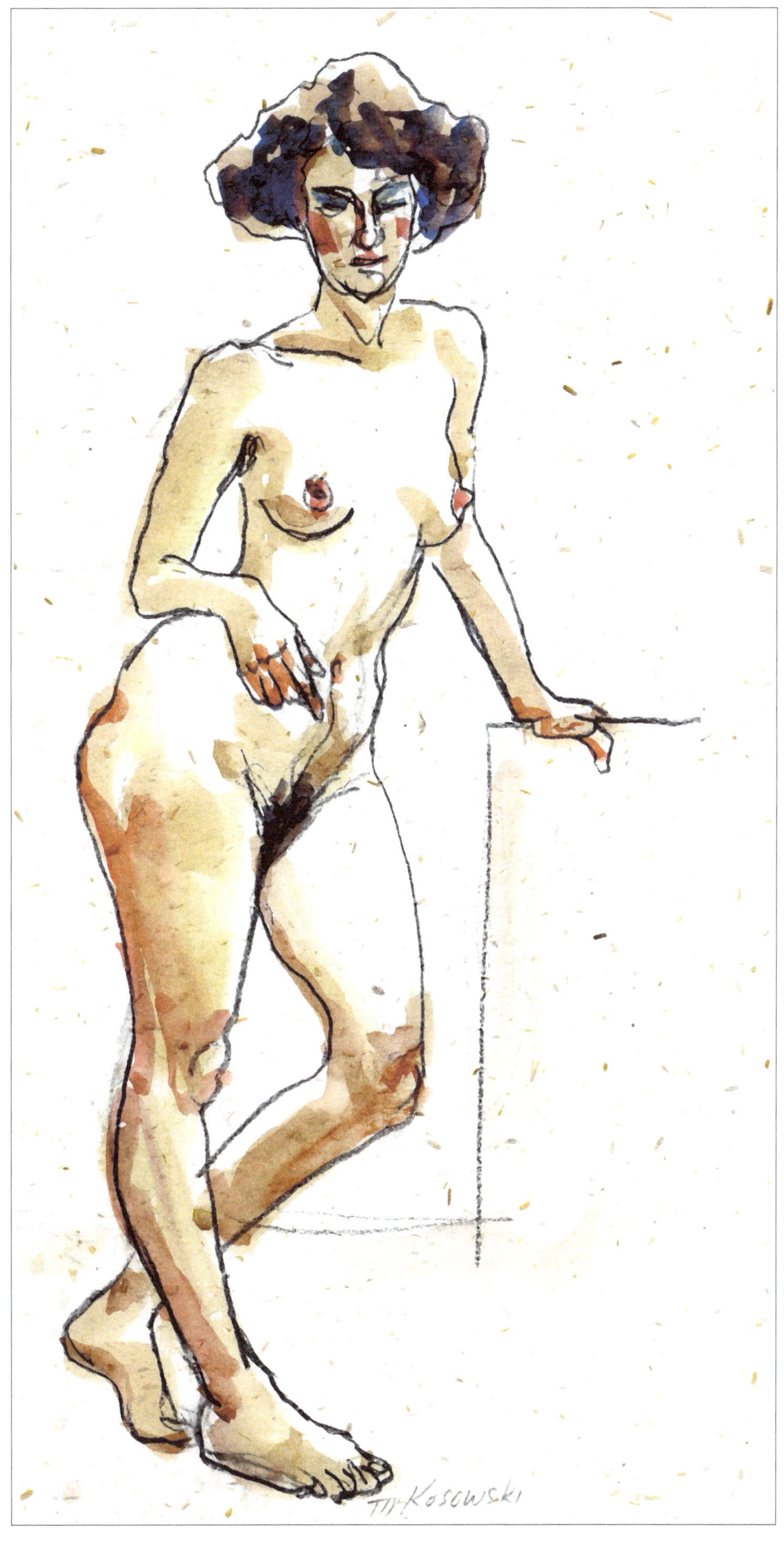
TM Kosowski

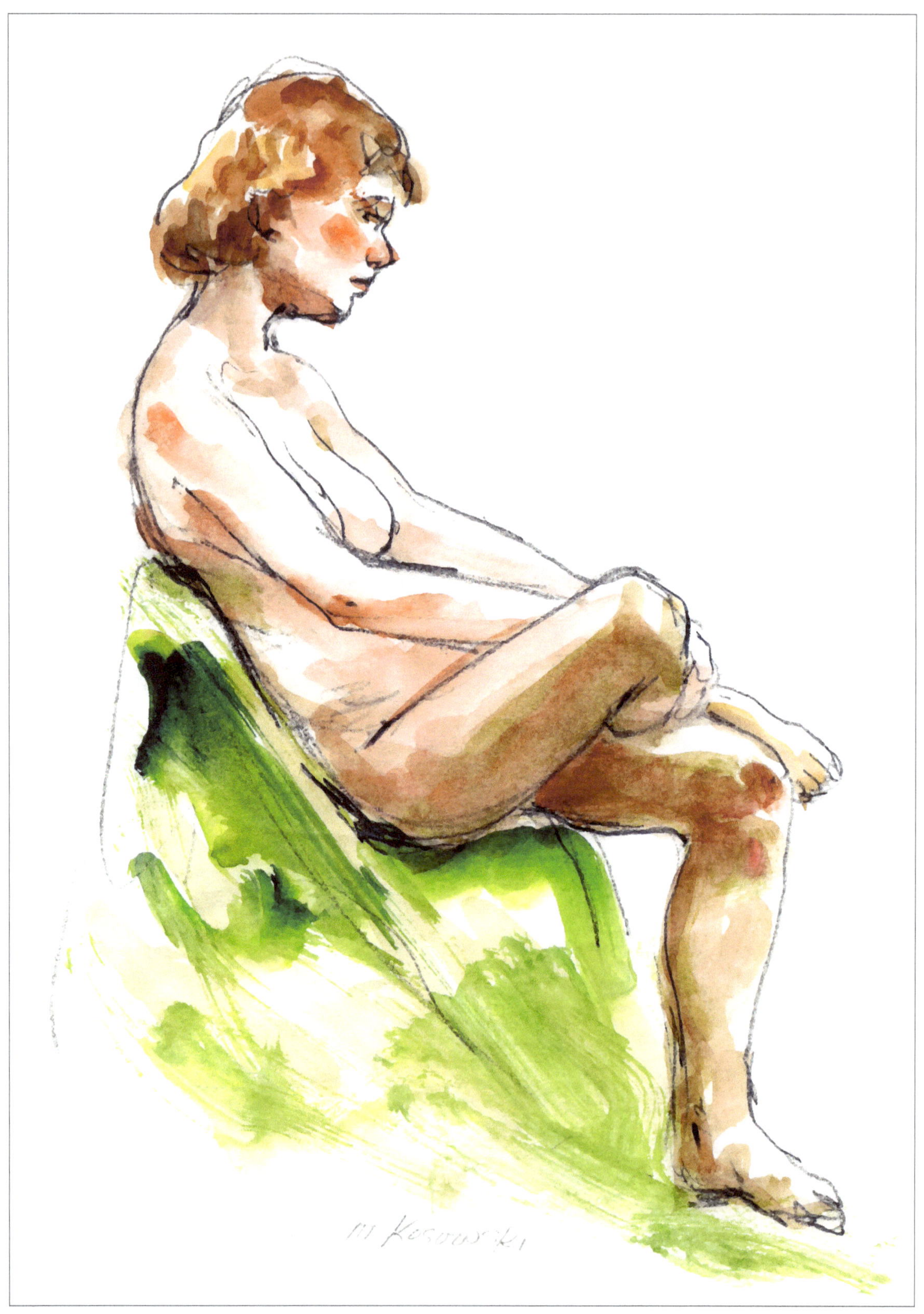

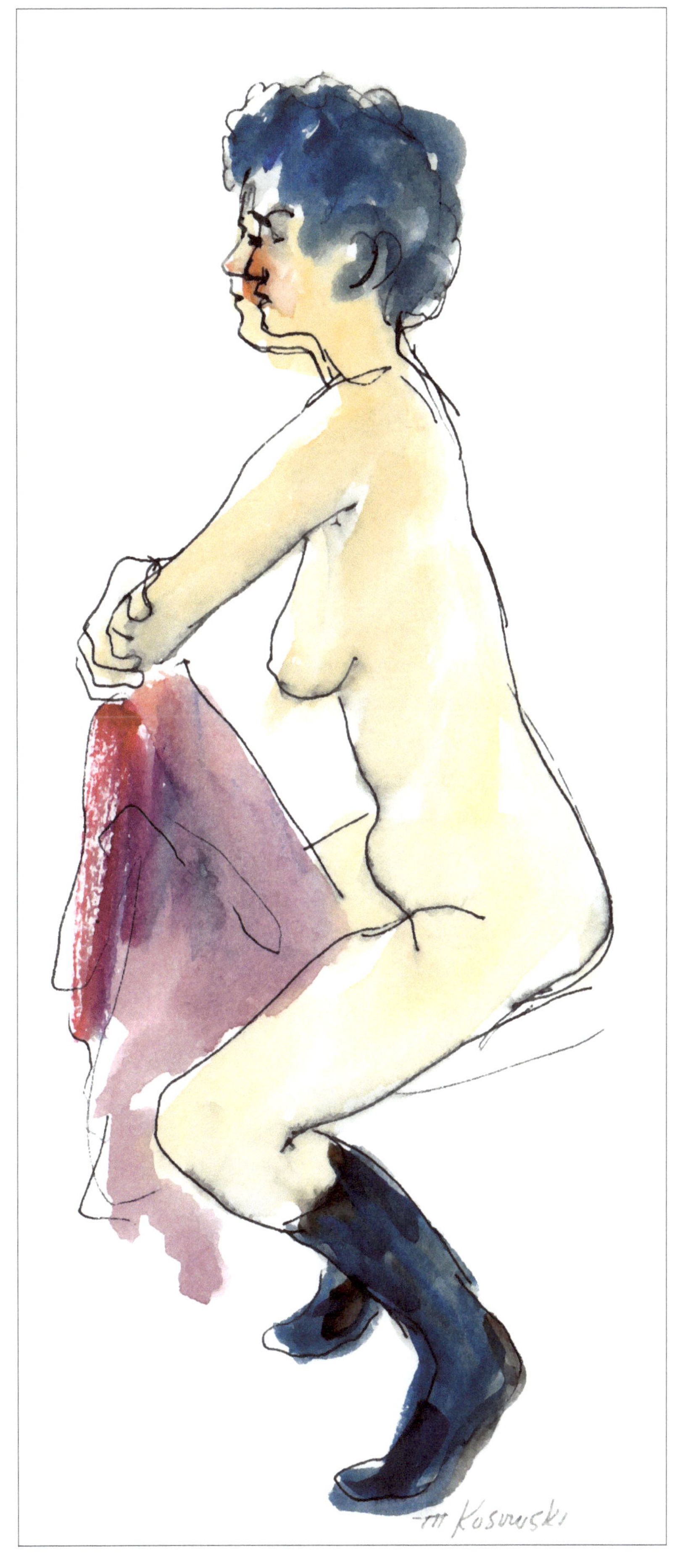
m Kosowski

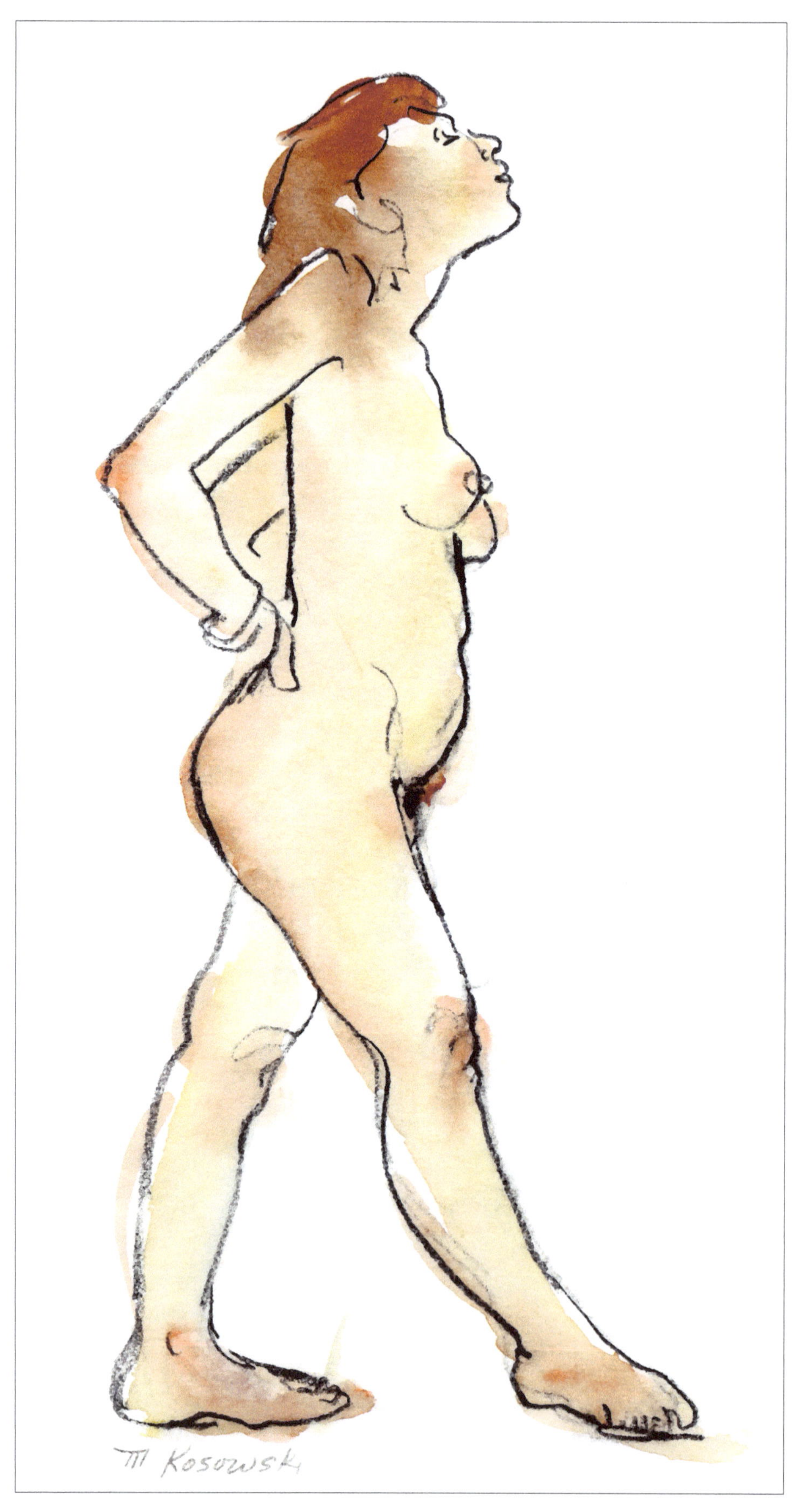
M Kosowsk

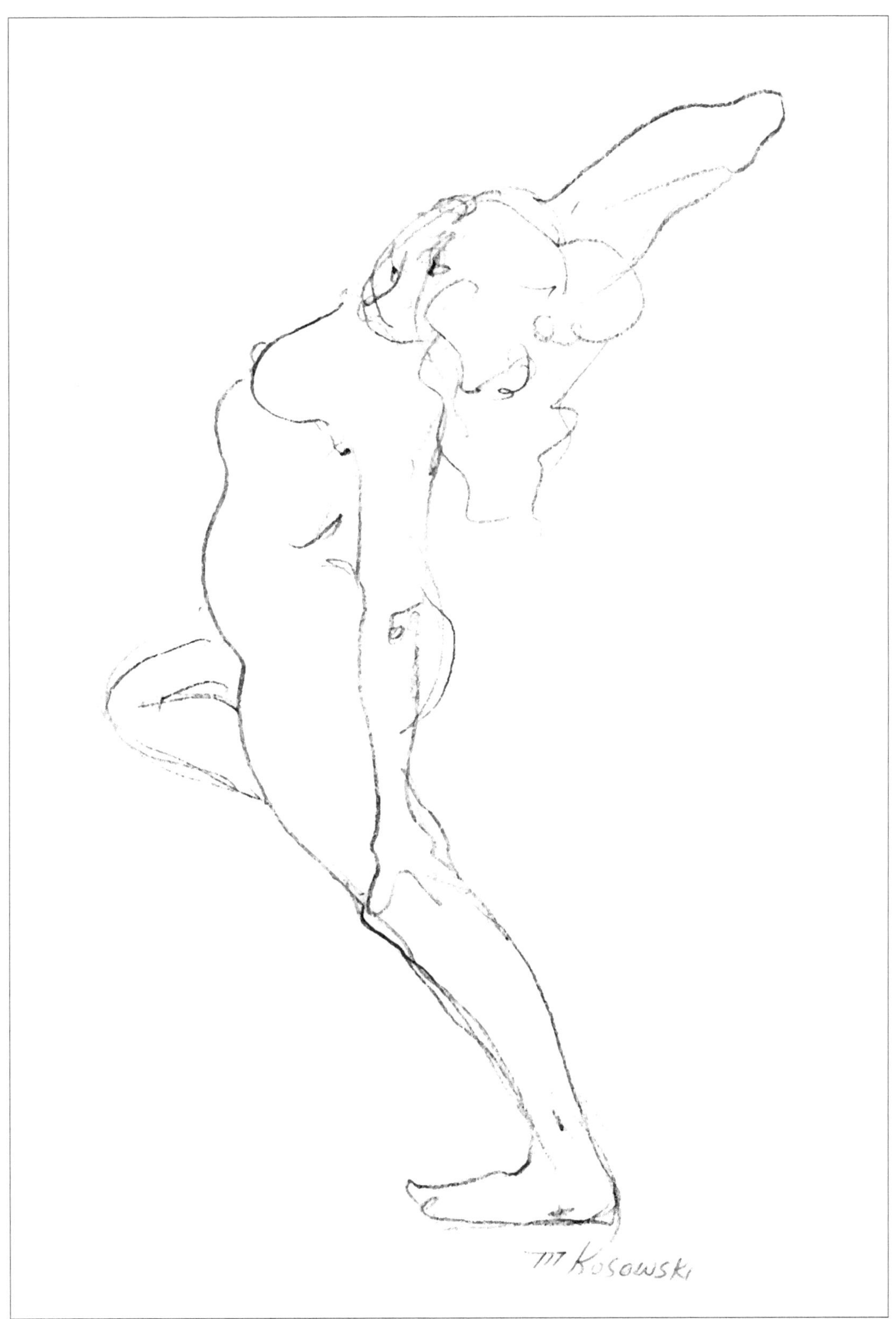
M Kosowski

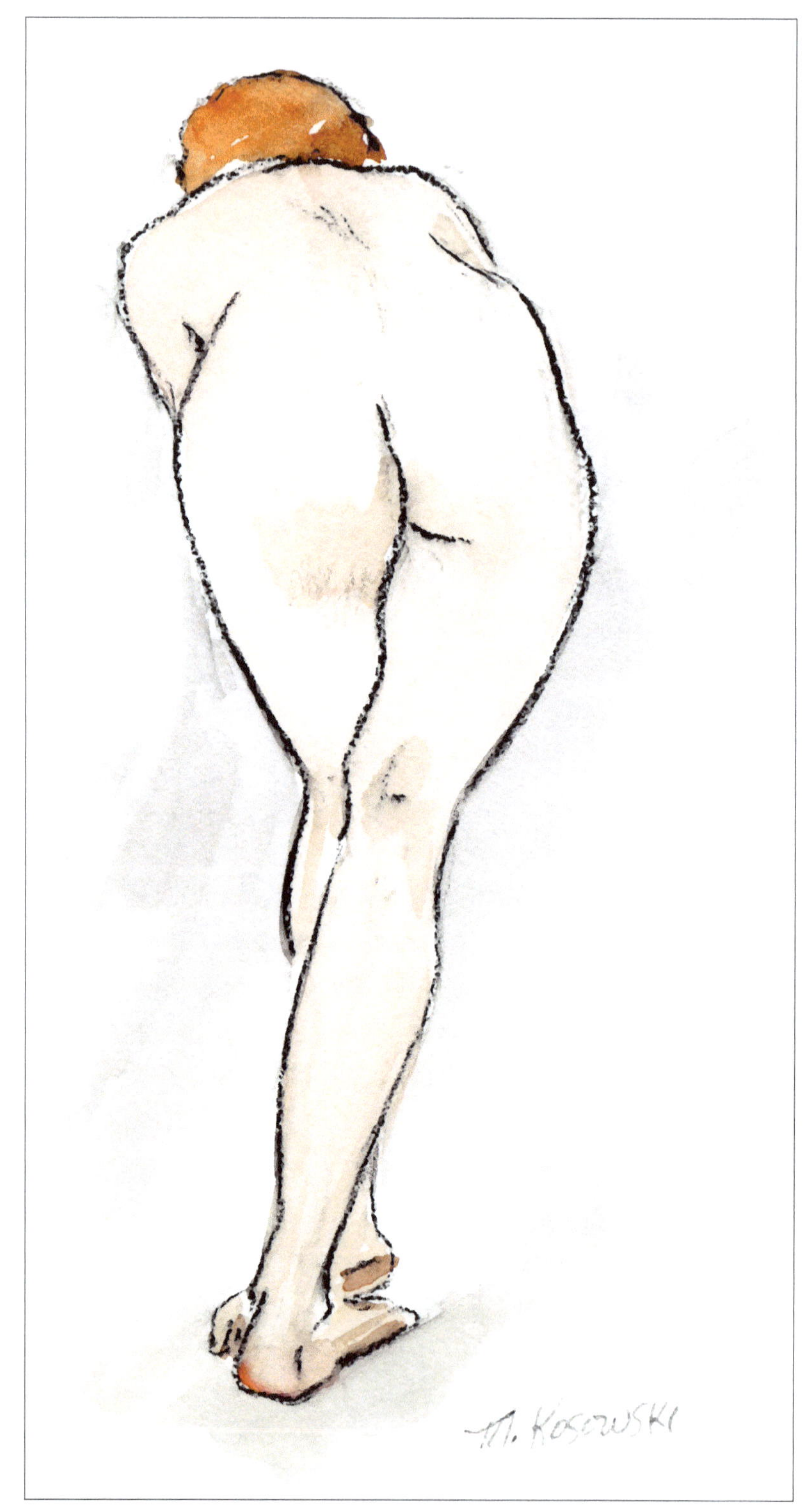
M. Kosowski

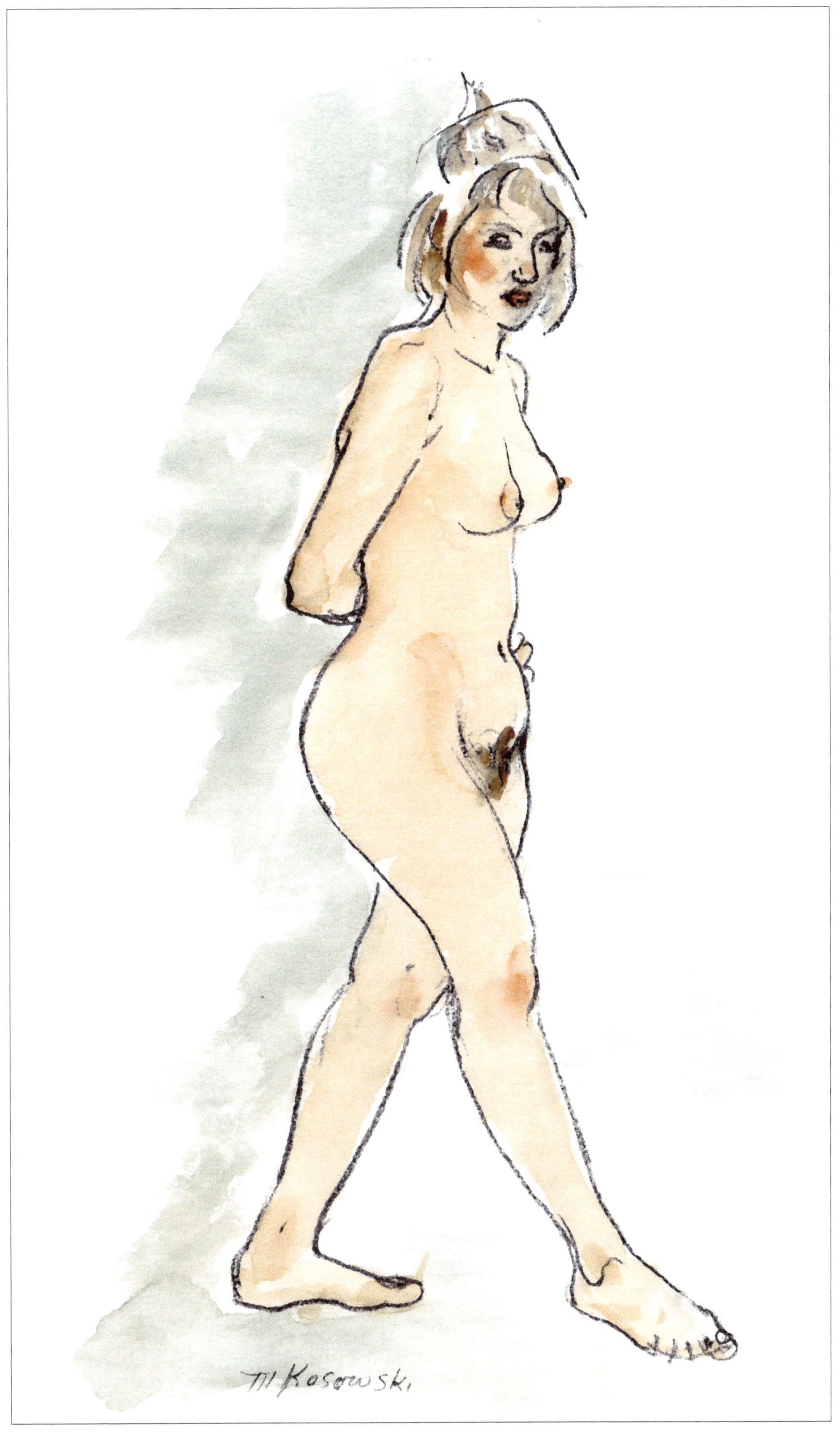
M Kosowski

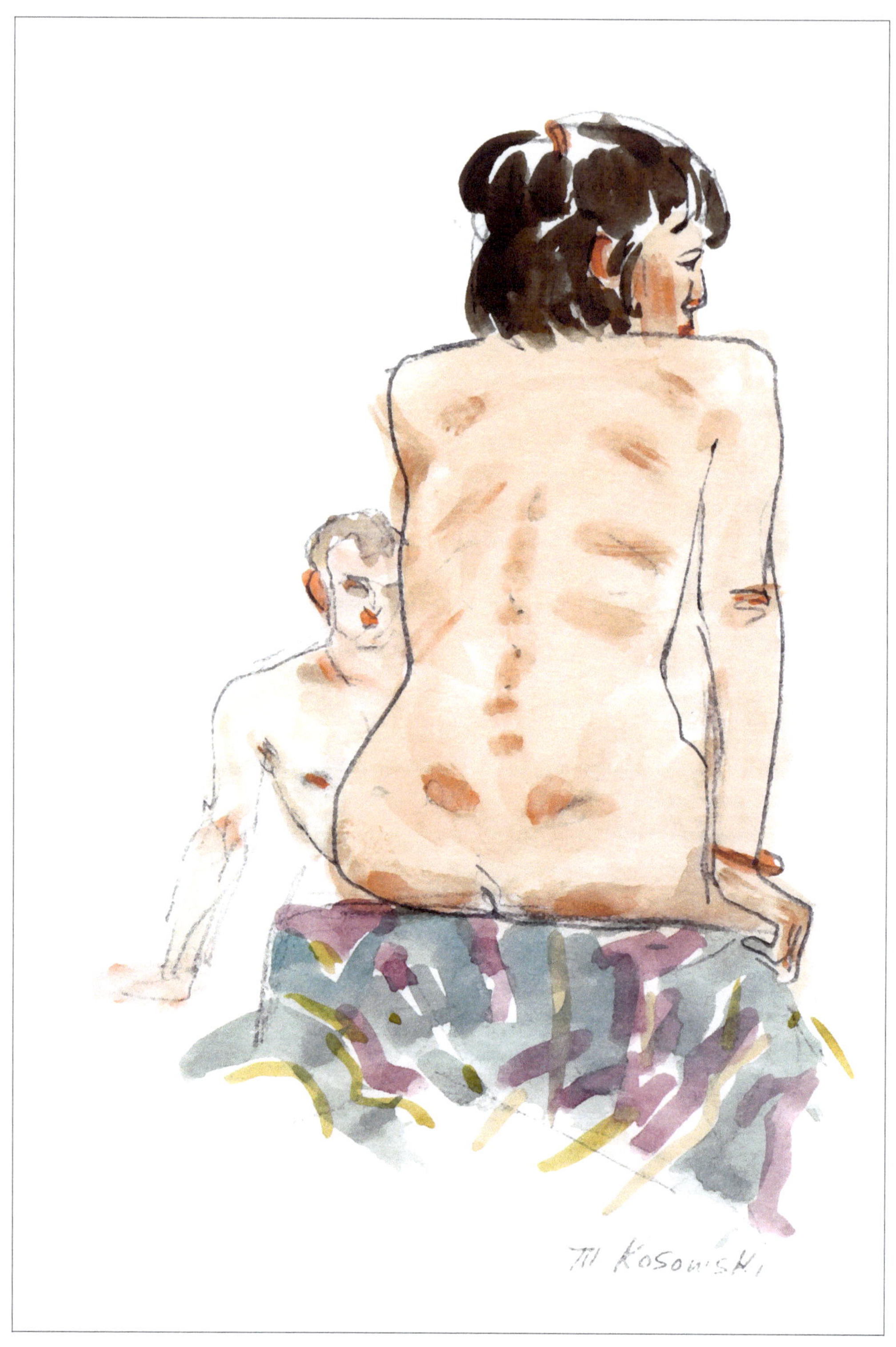

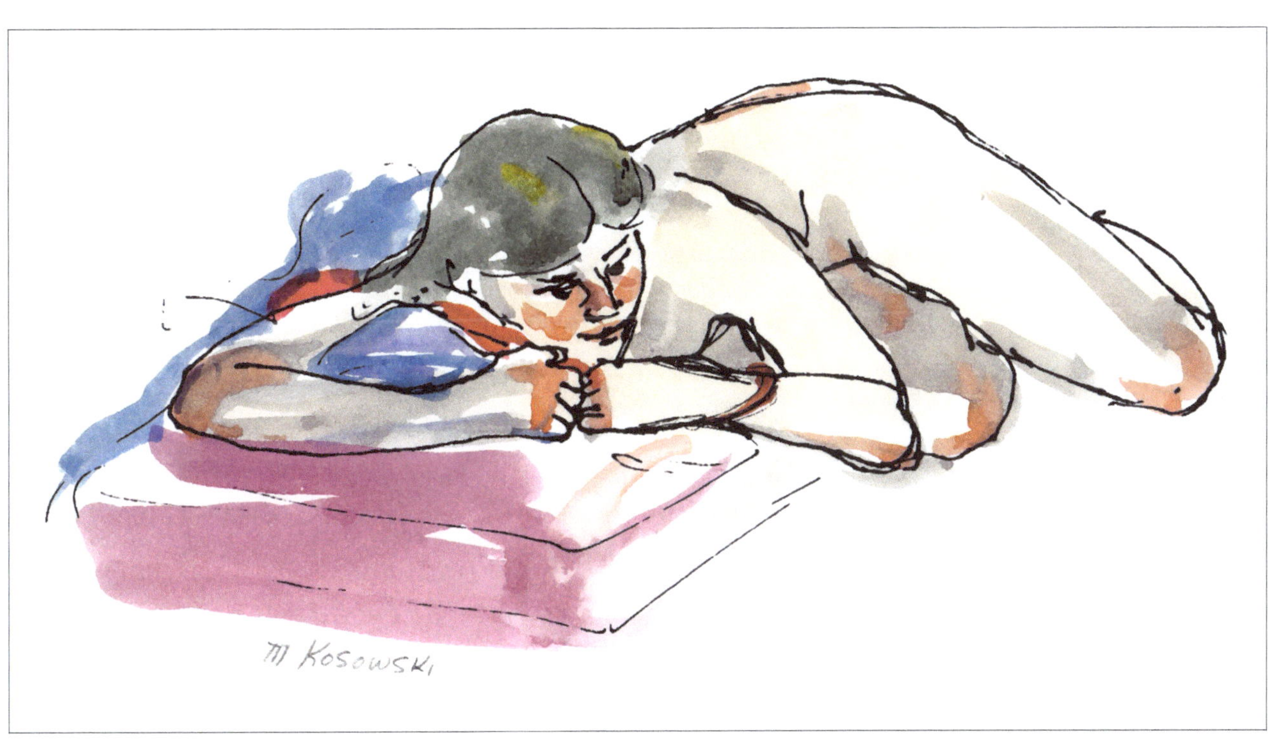
M Kosowski

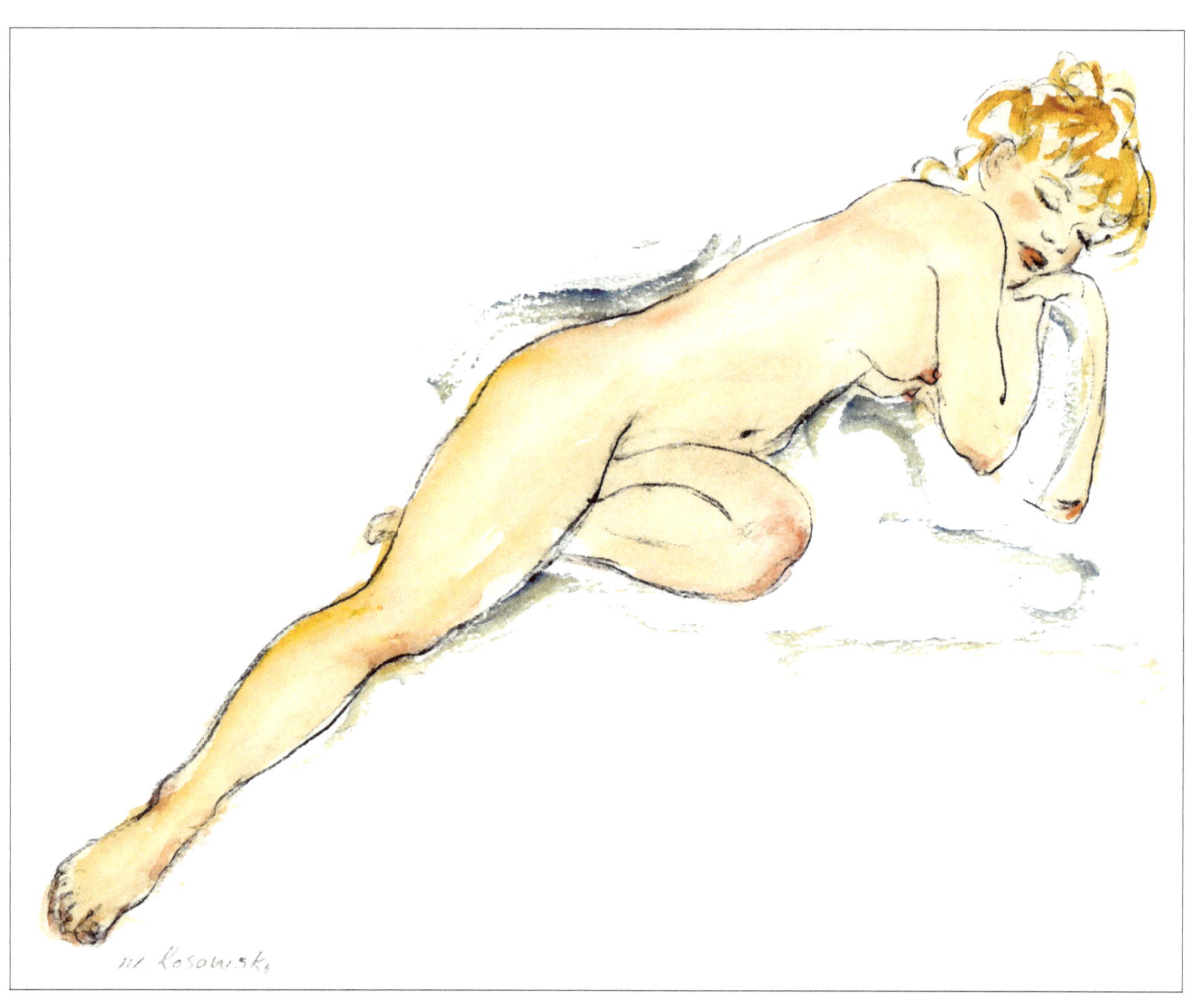

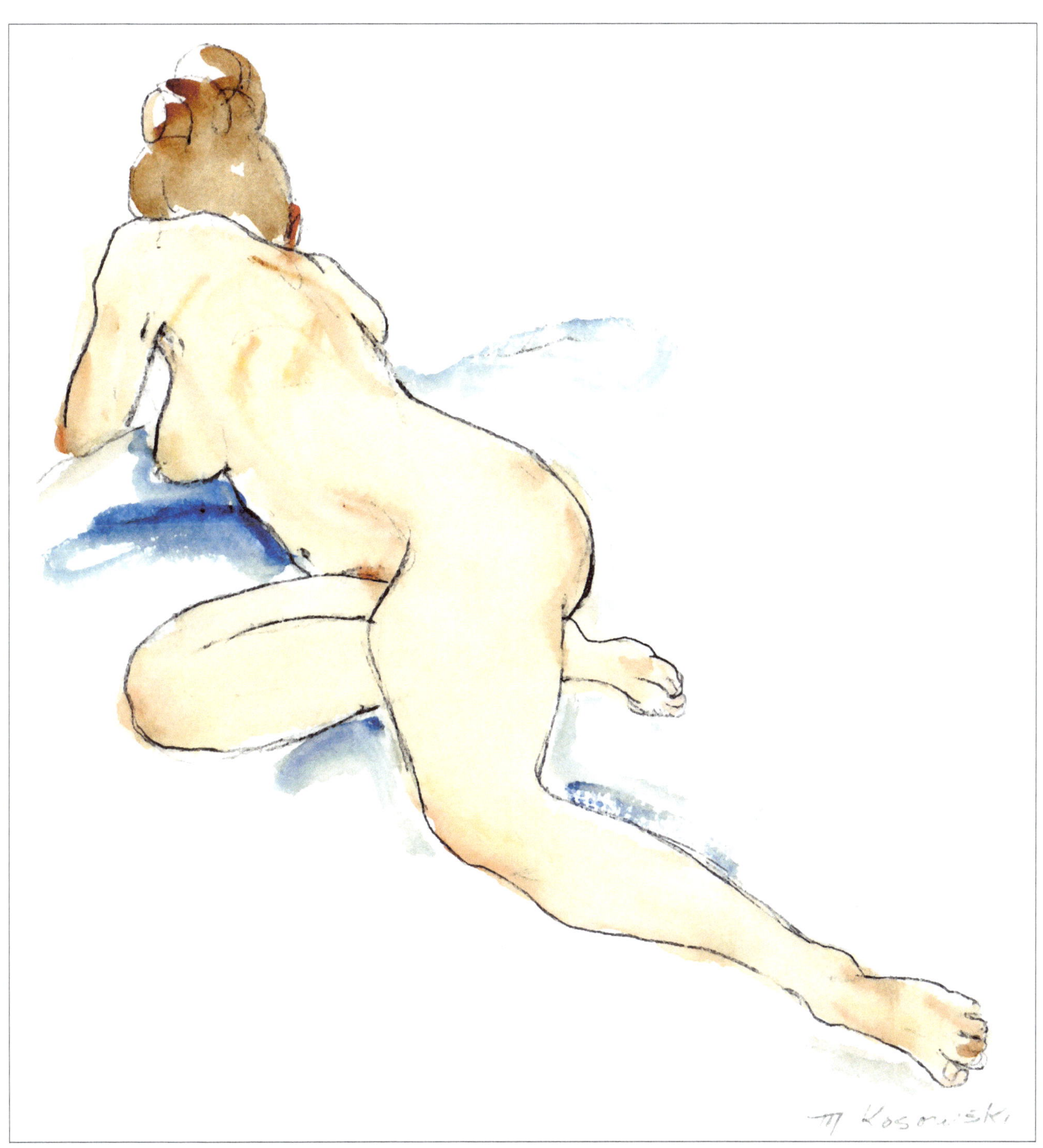
M Kosowski

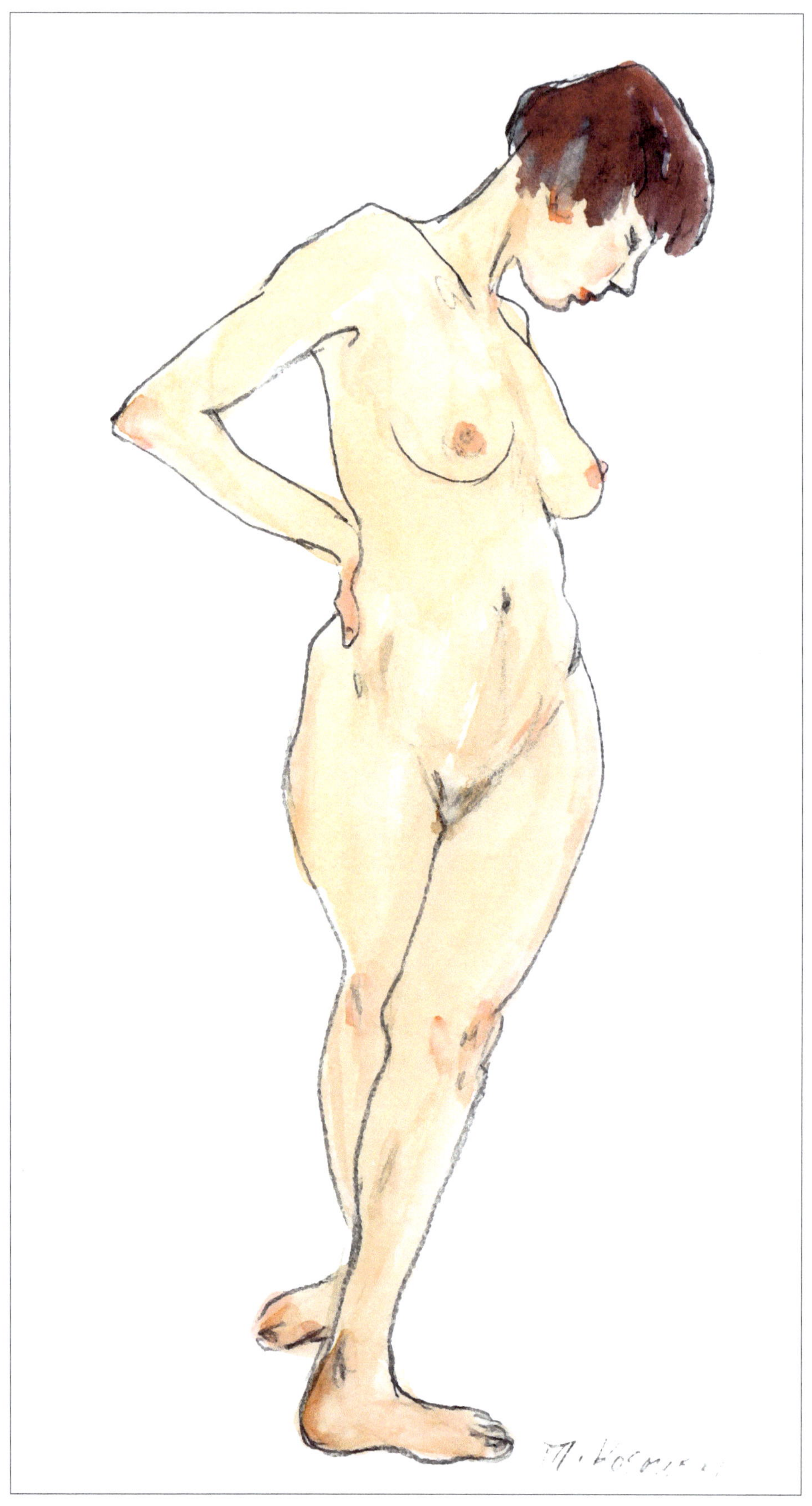

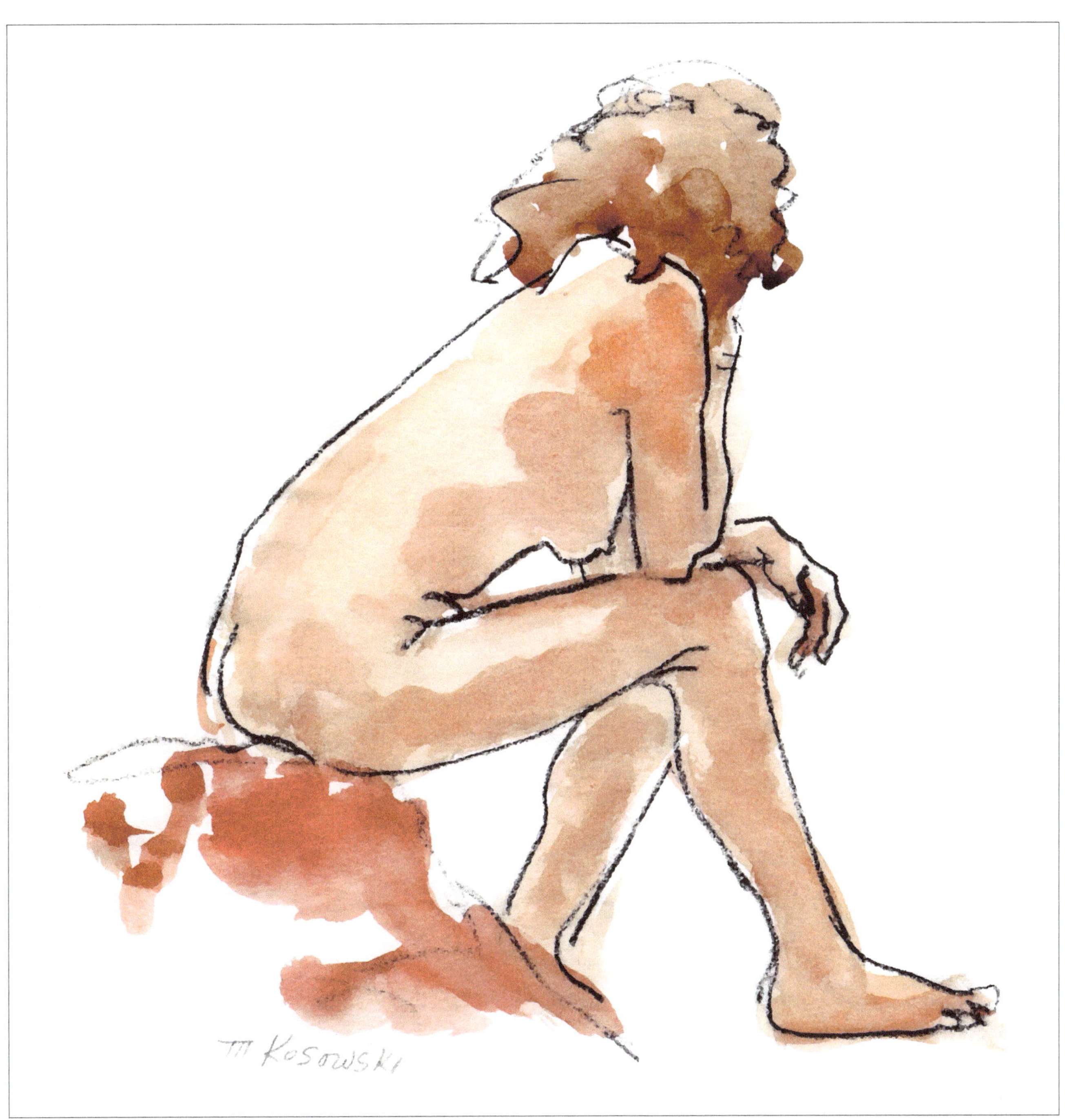
TM KOSOWSKI

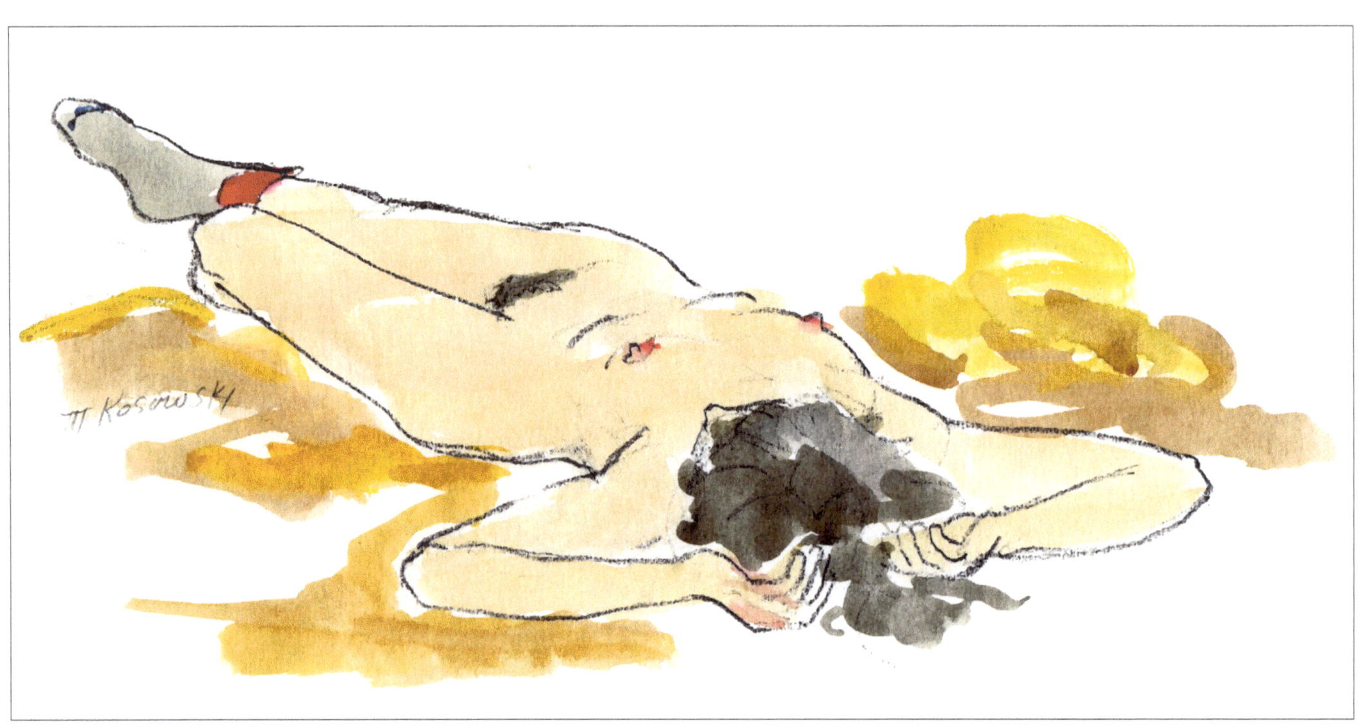

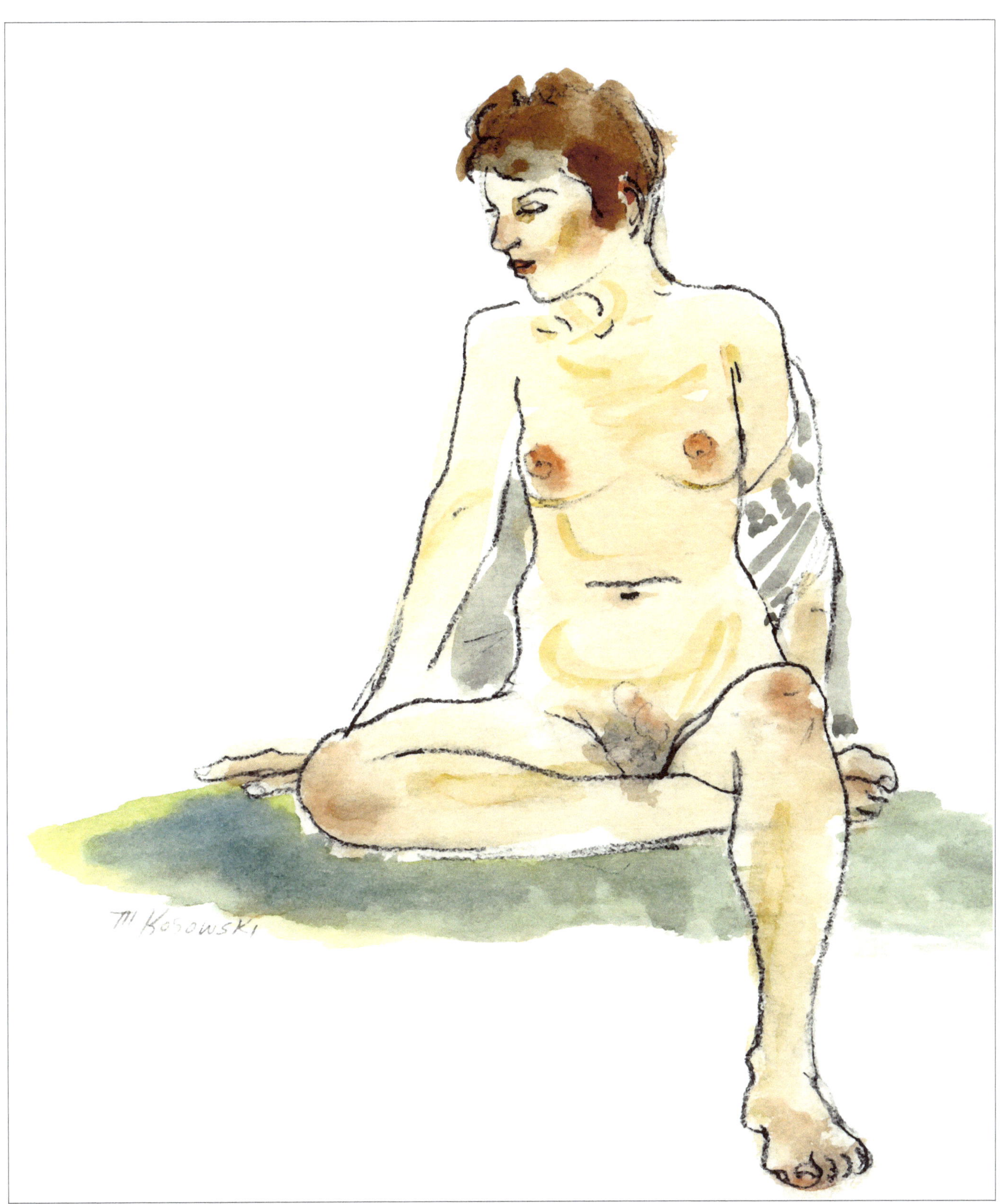
M Kosowski

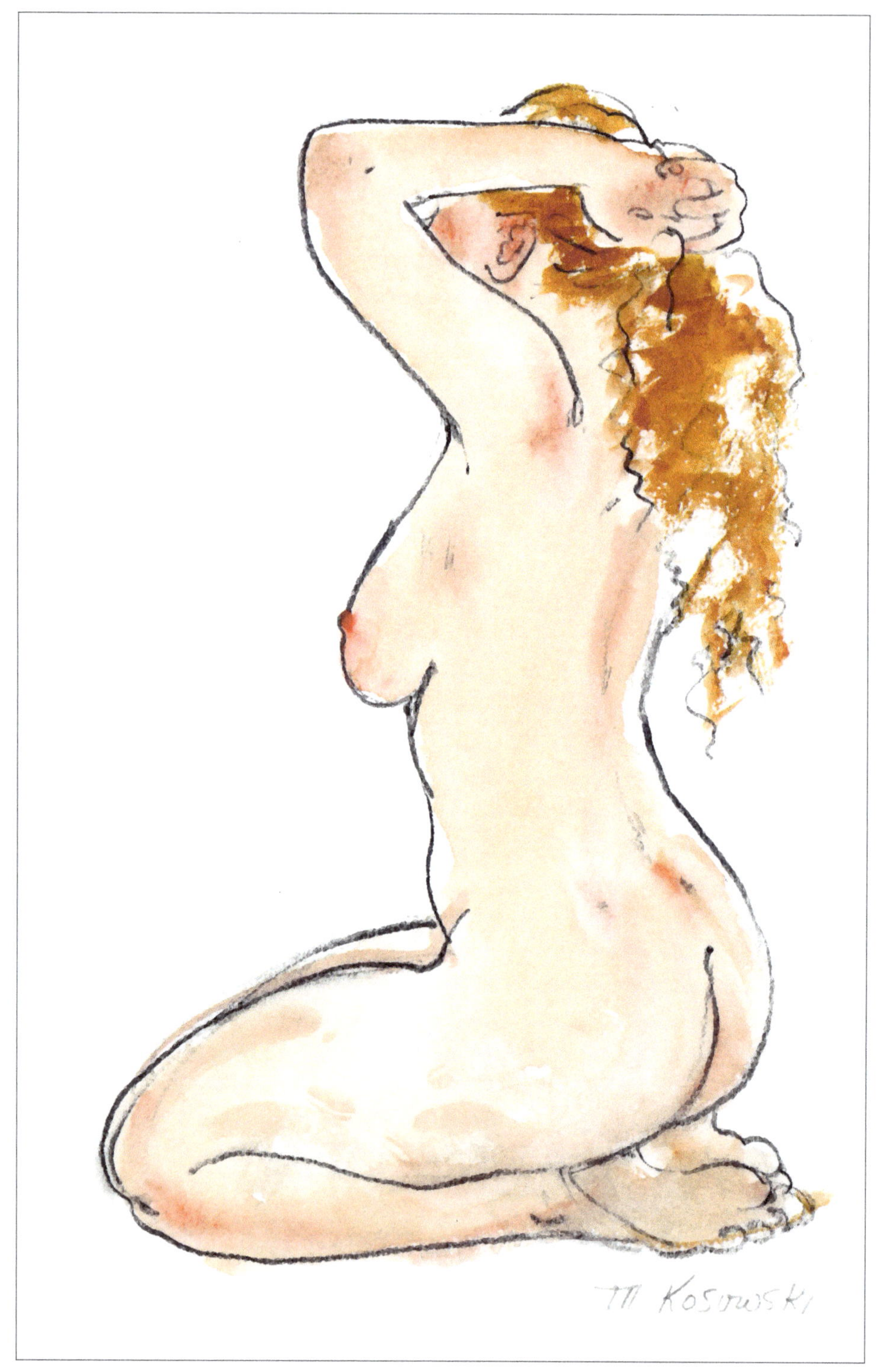
M Kosowski

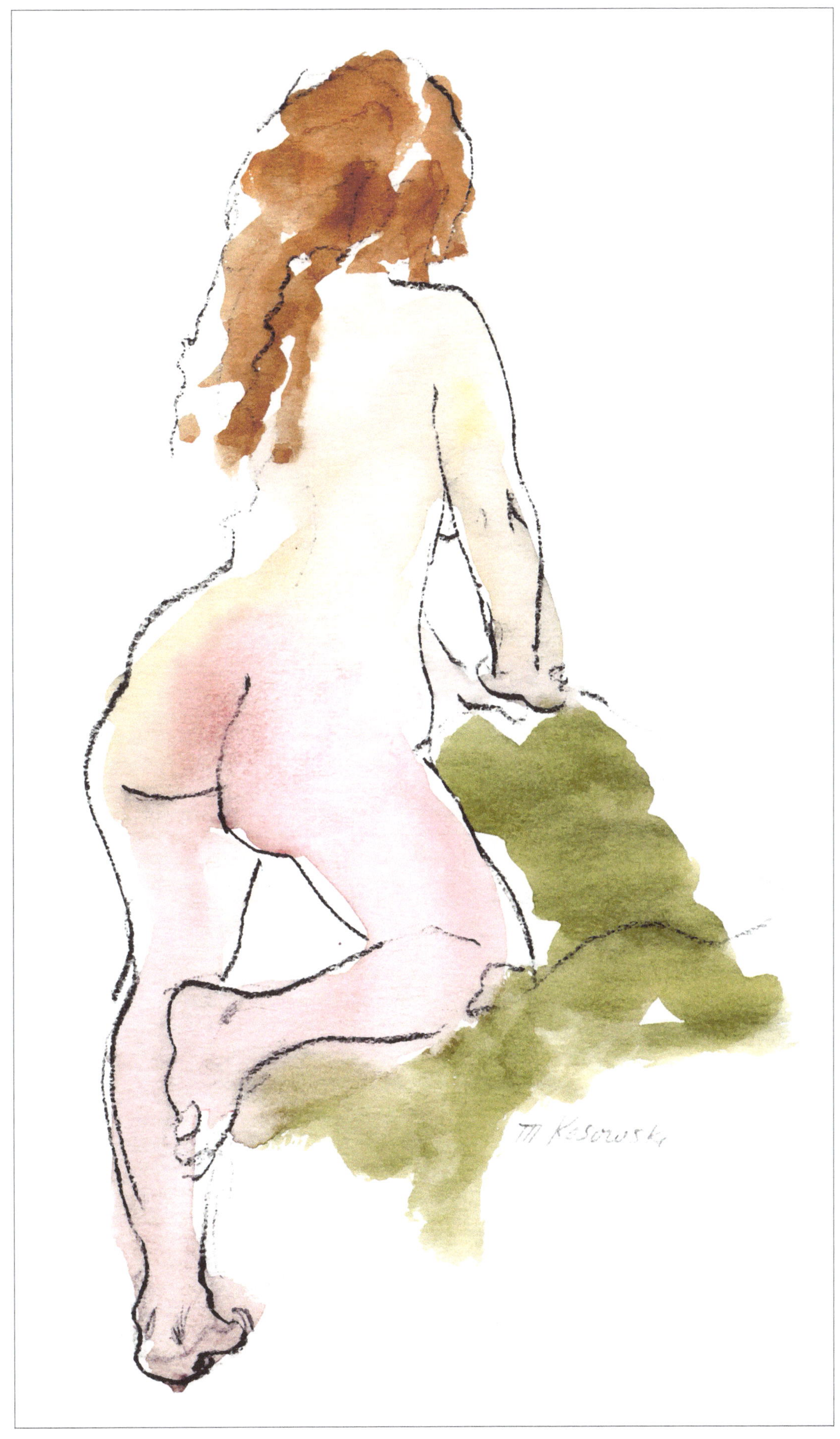
M Kosowski

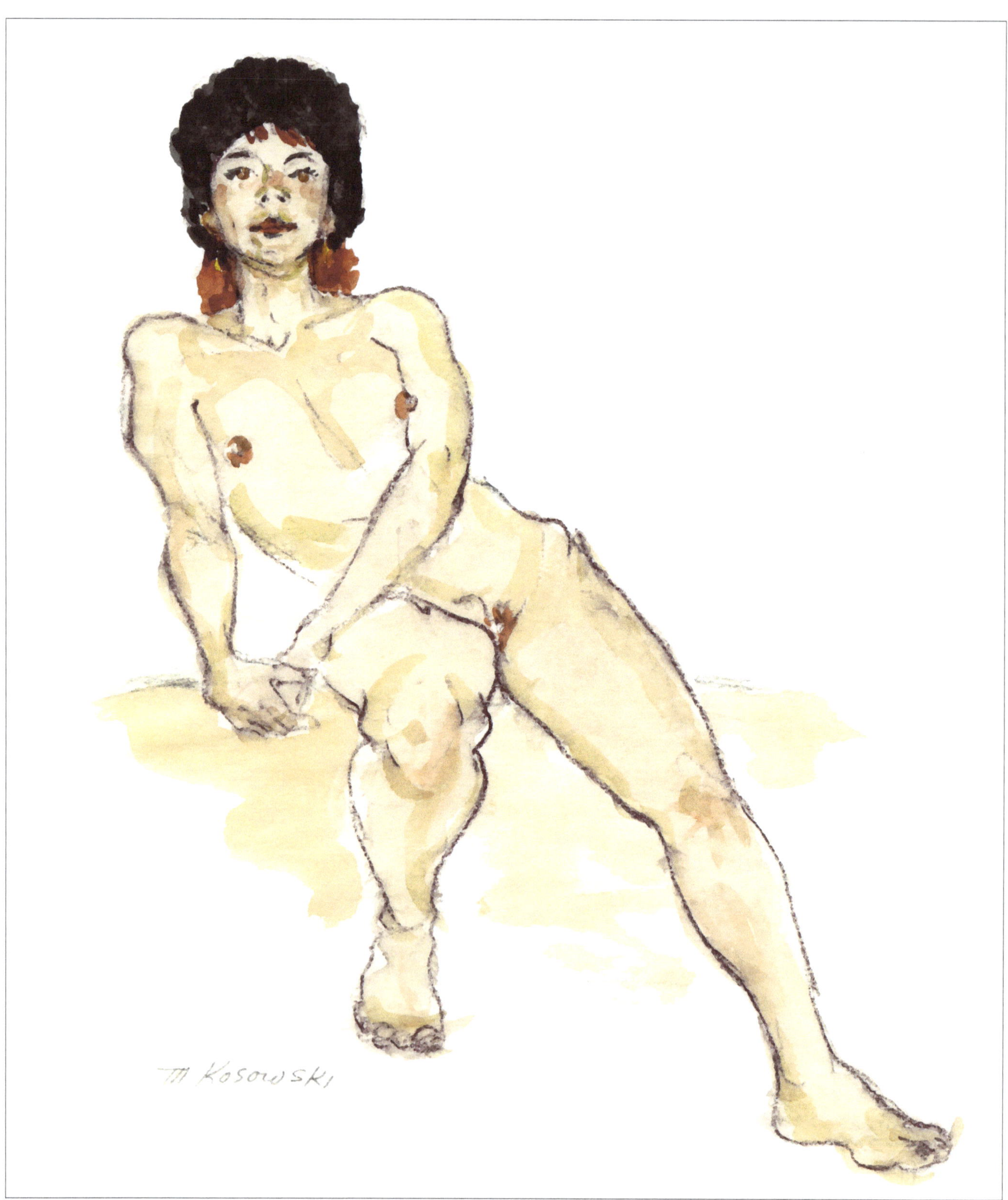
M Kosowski

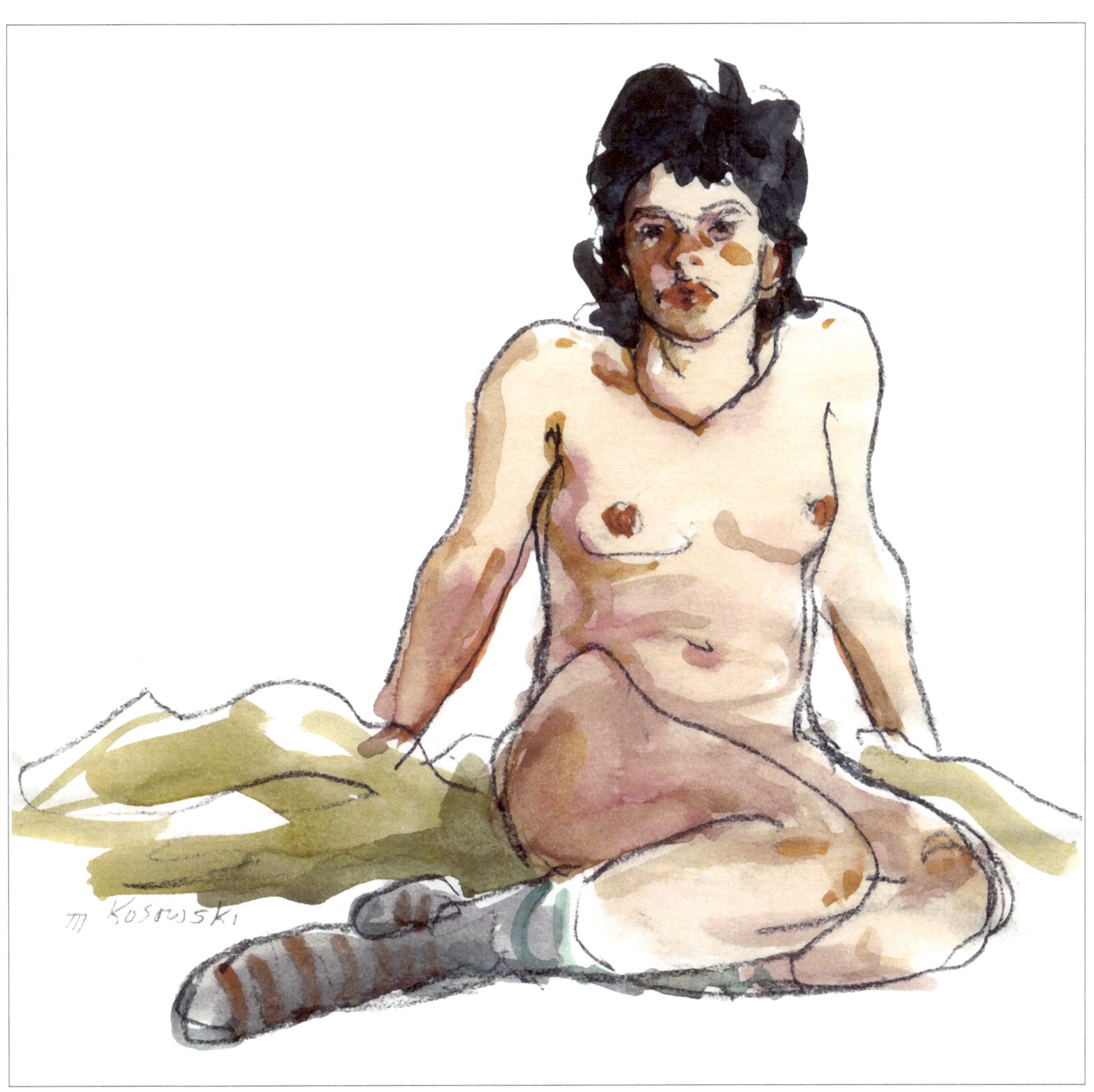
m Kosowski

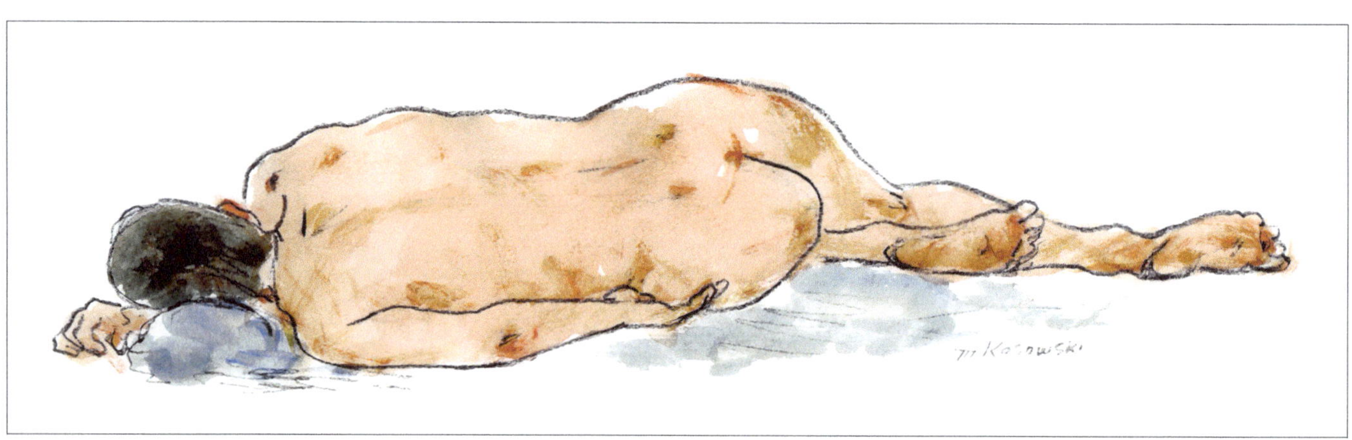

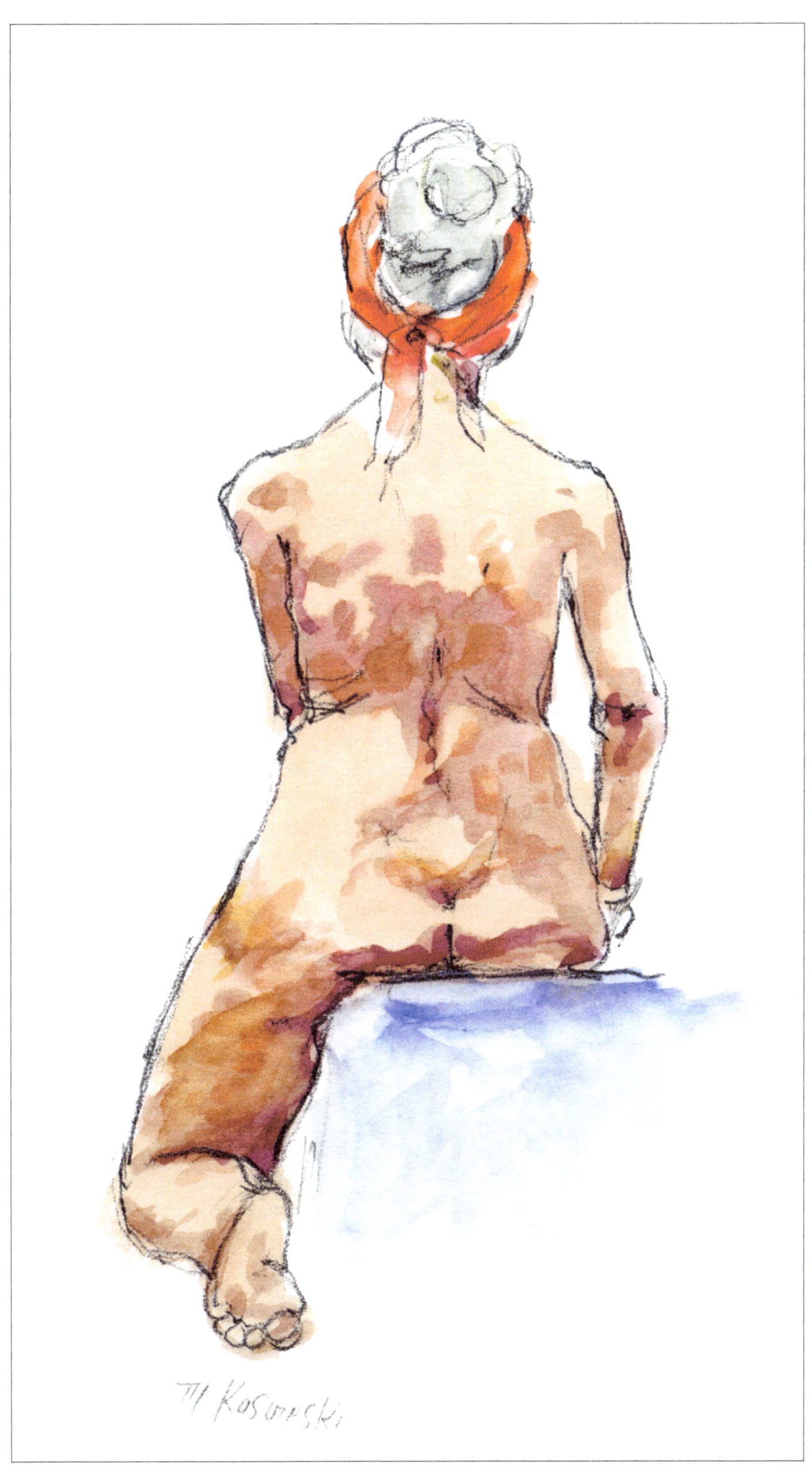

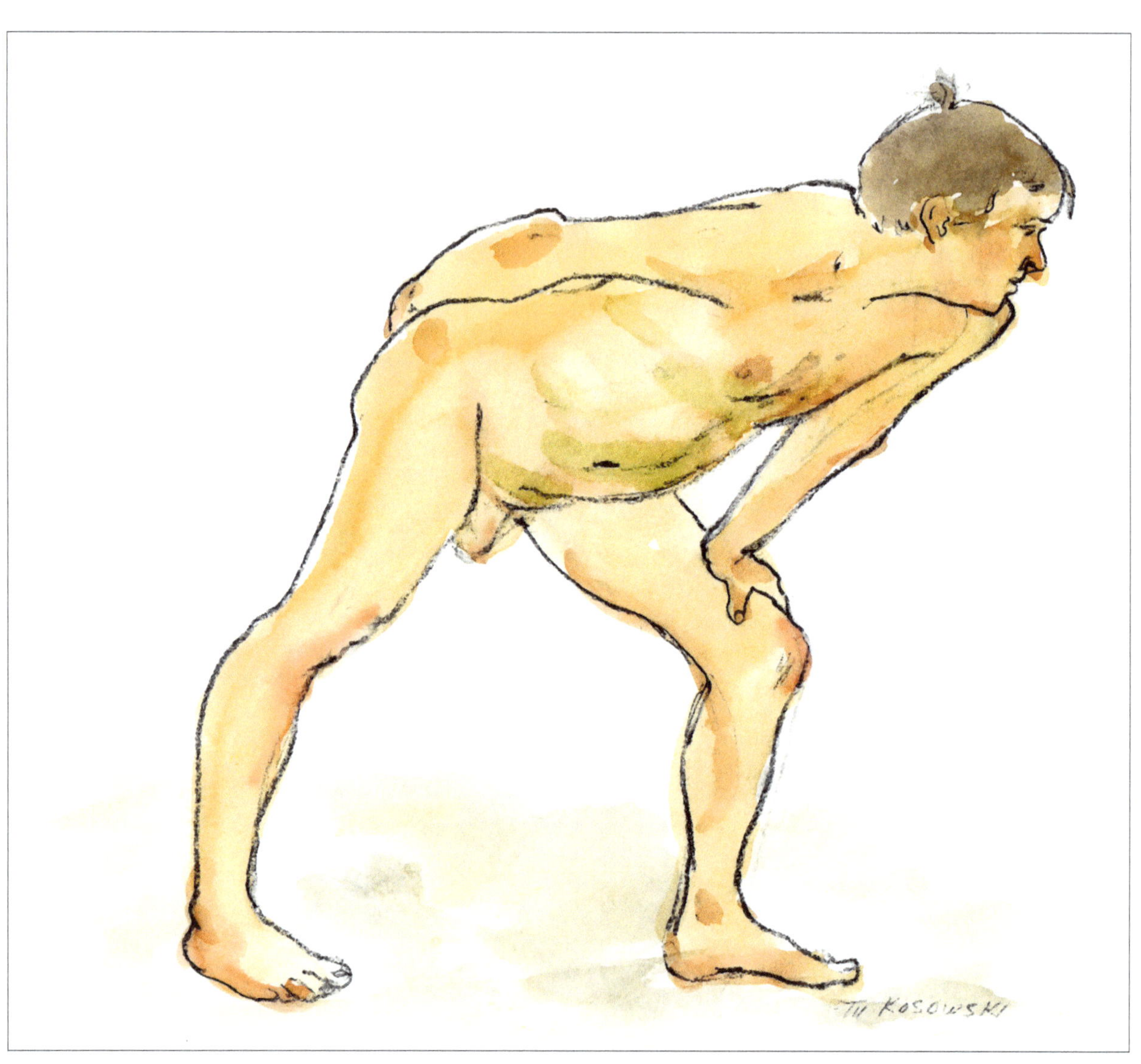
TU KOSOWSKI

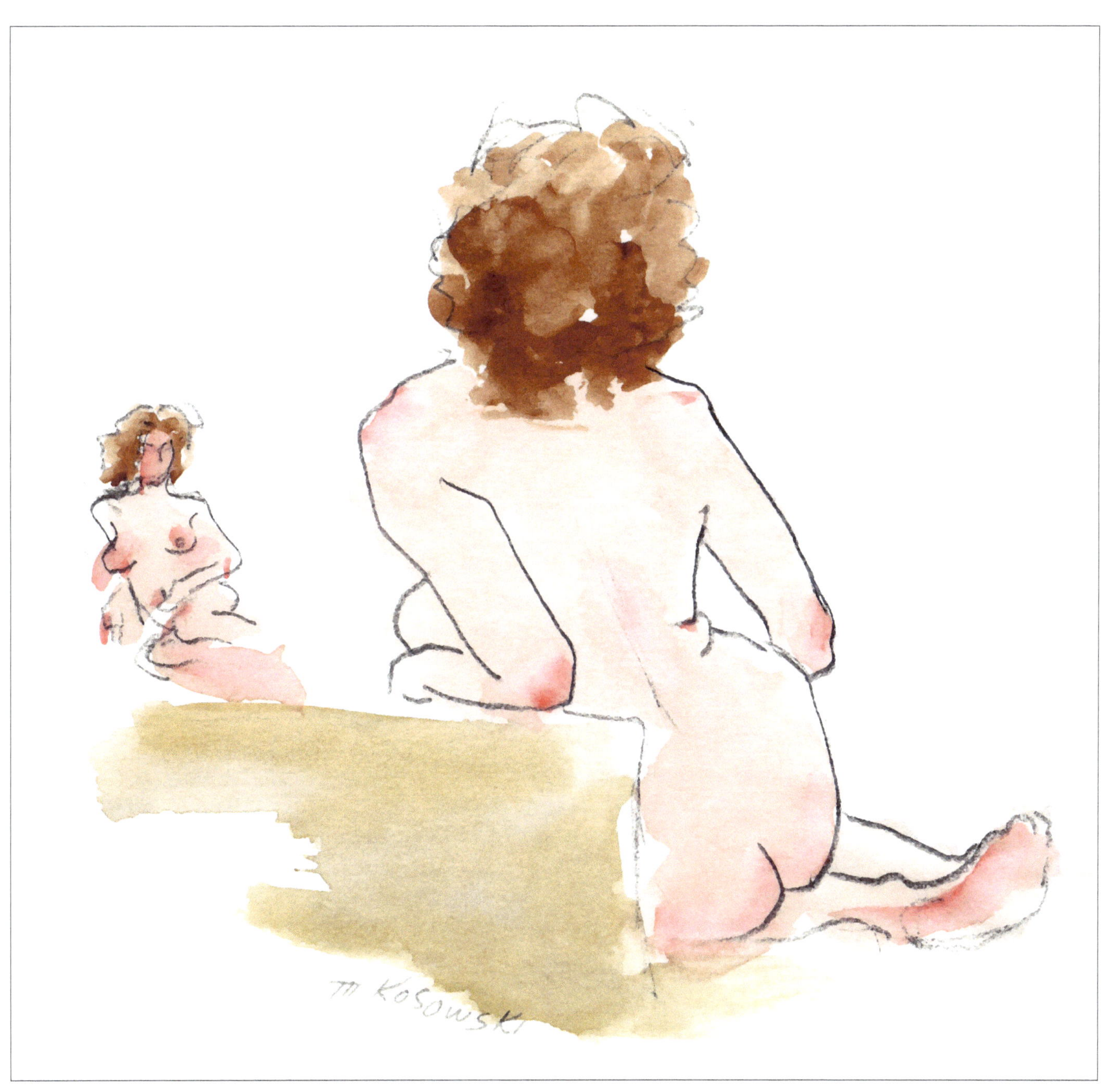
m KOSOWSKI

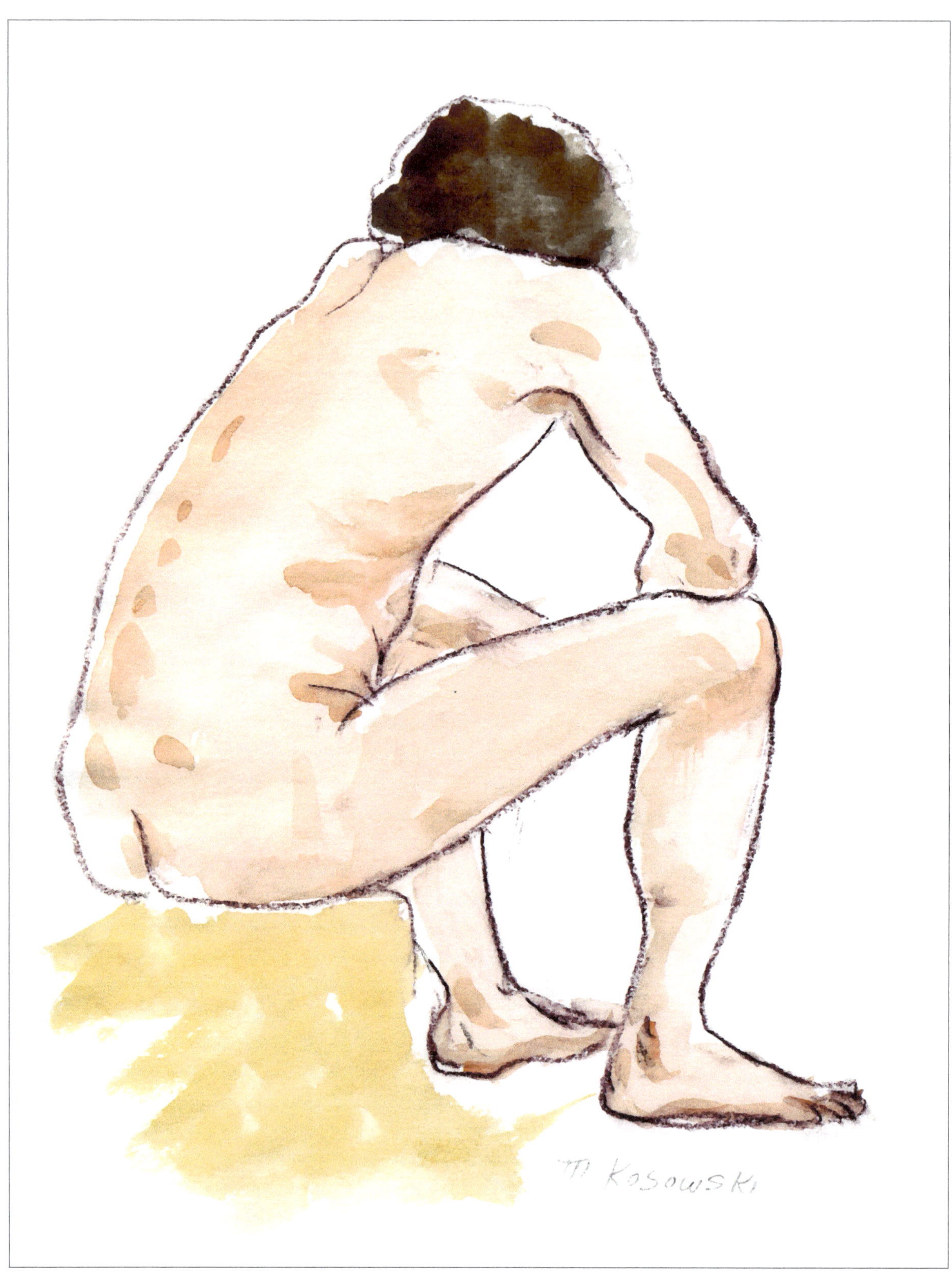
Kosowski

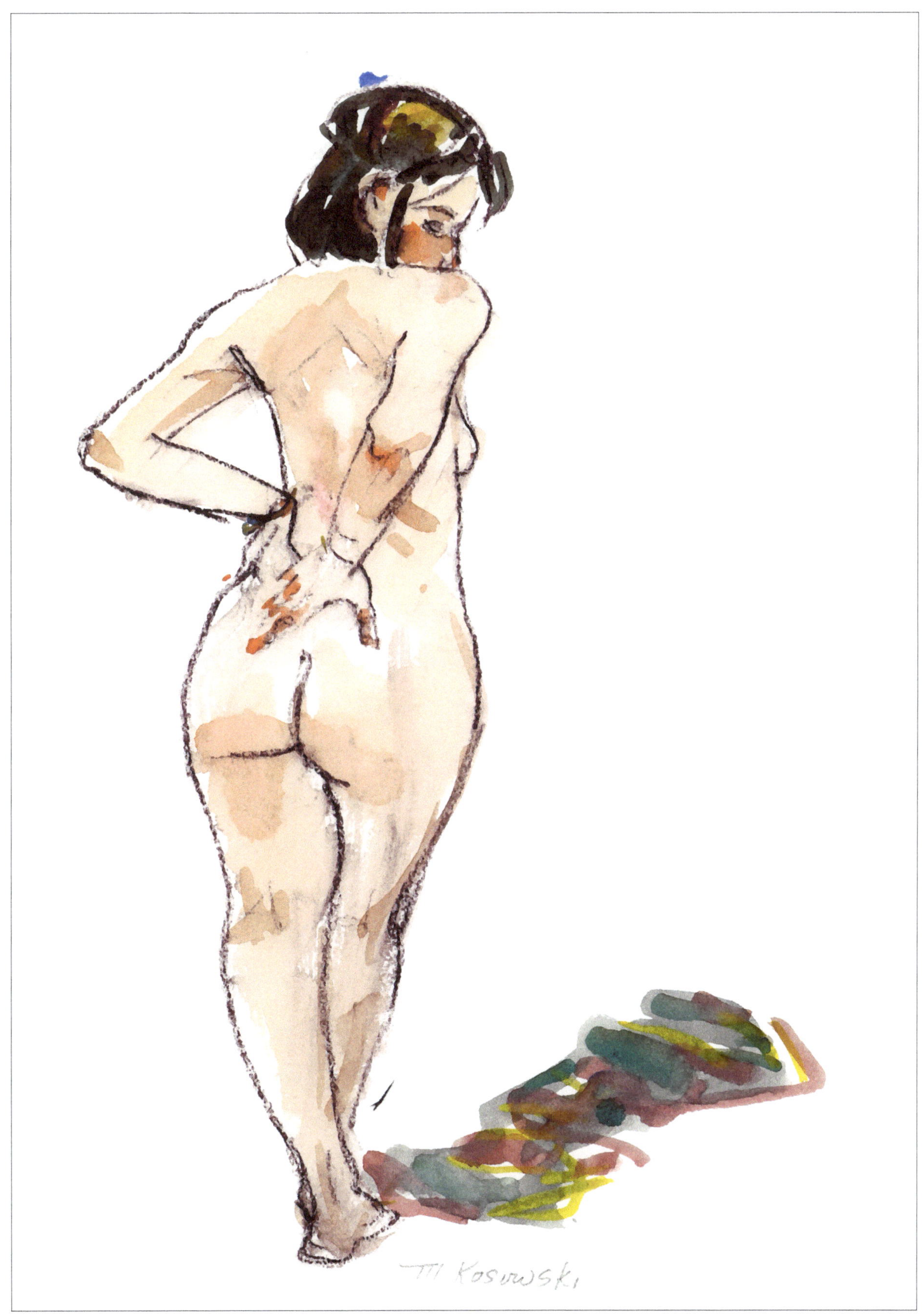
TM Kosowski

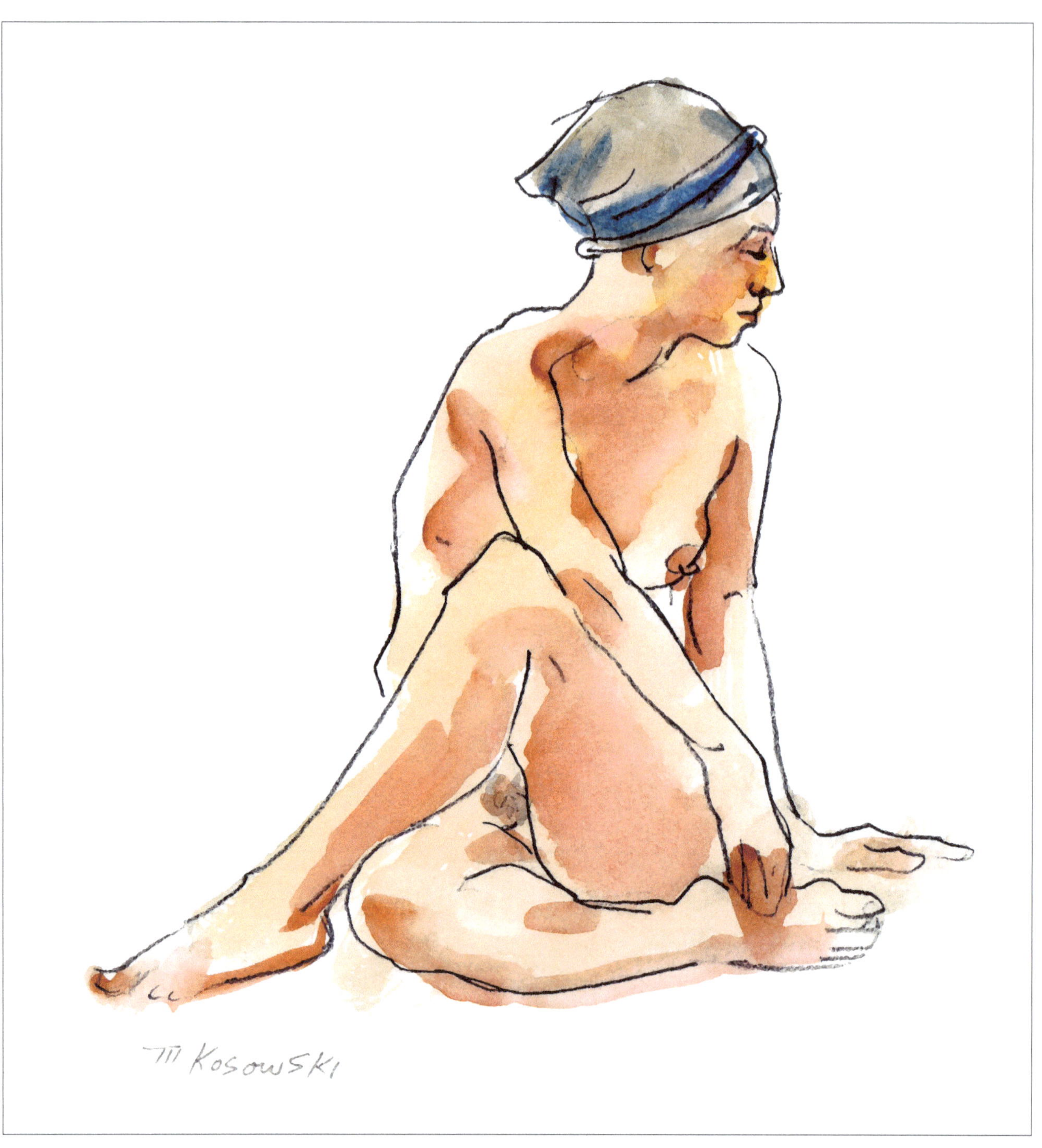
M Kosowski

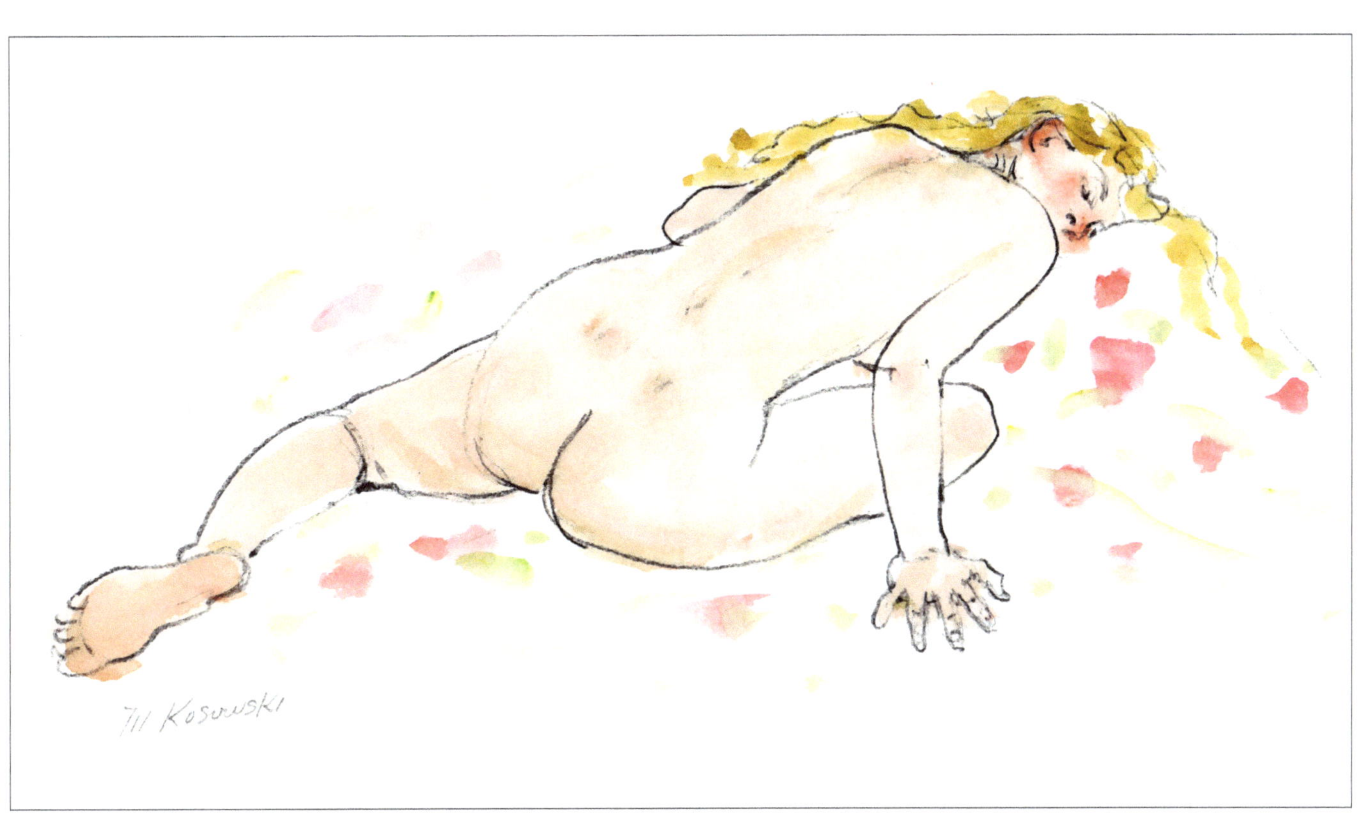
Jill Kosowski

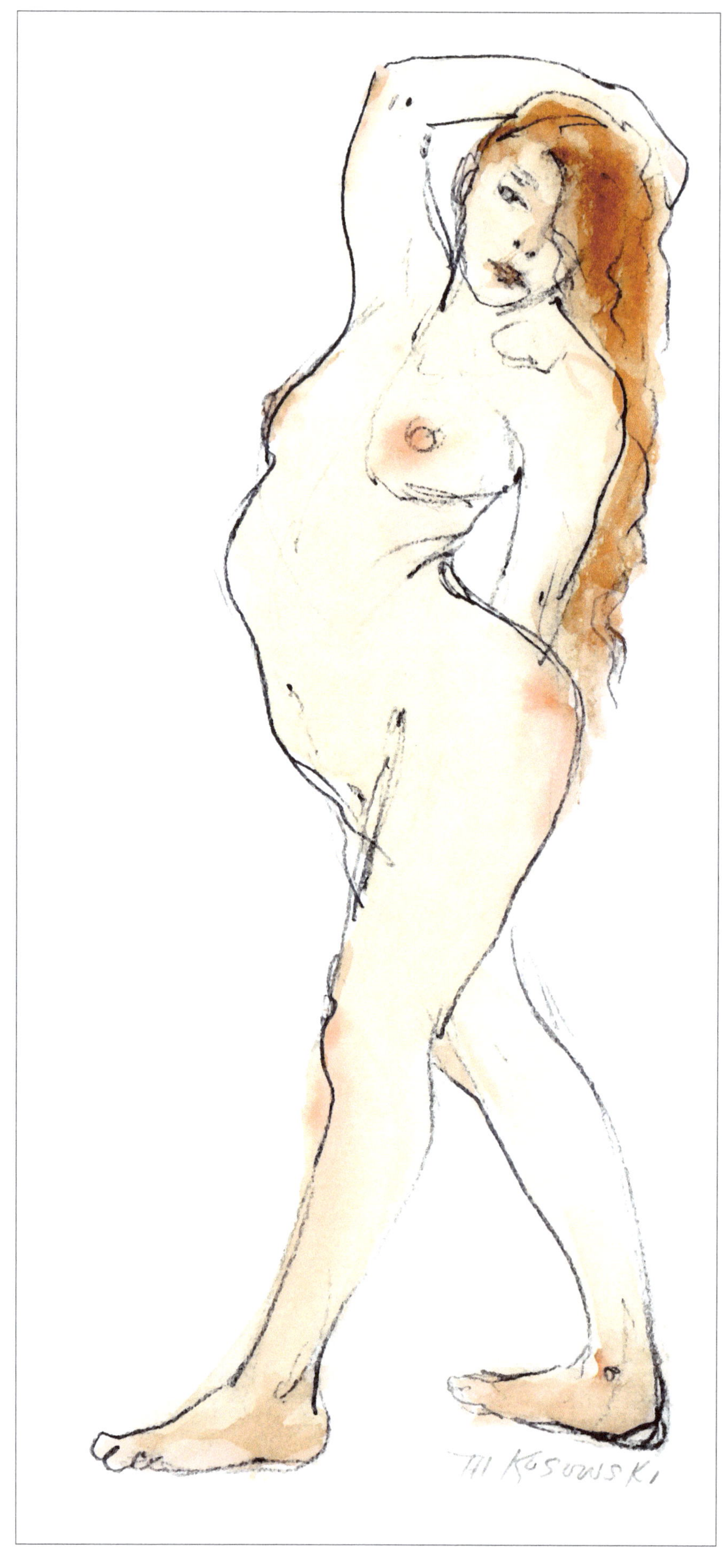

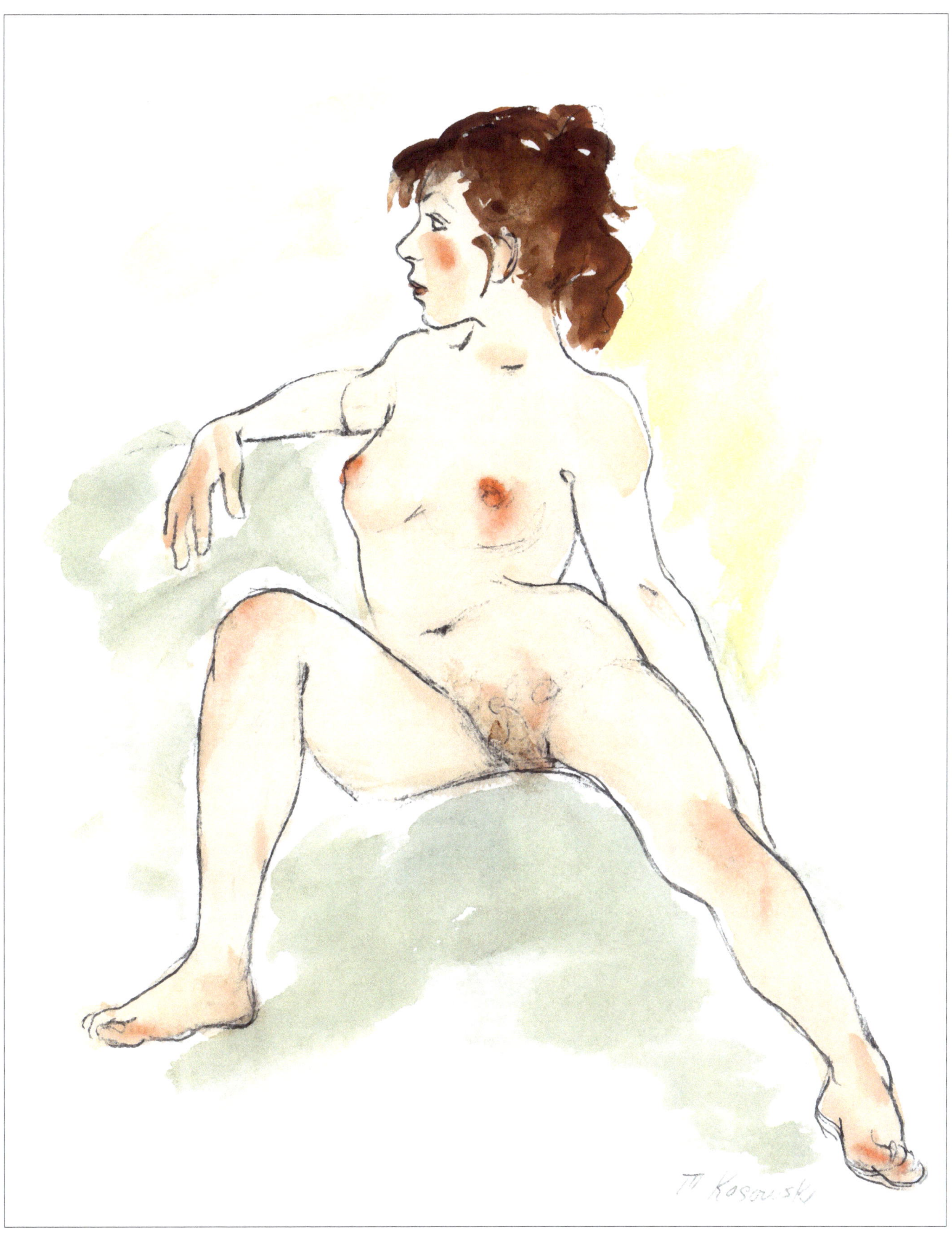

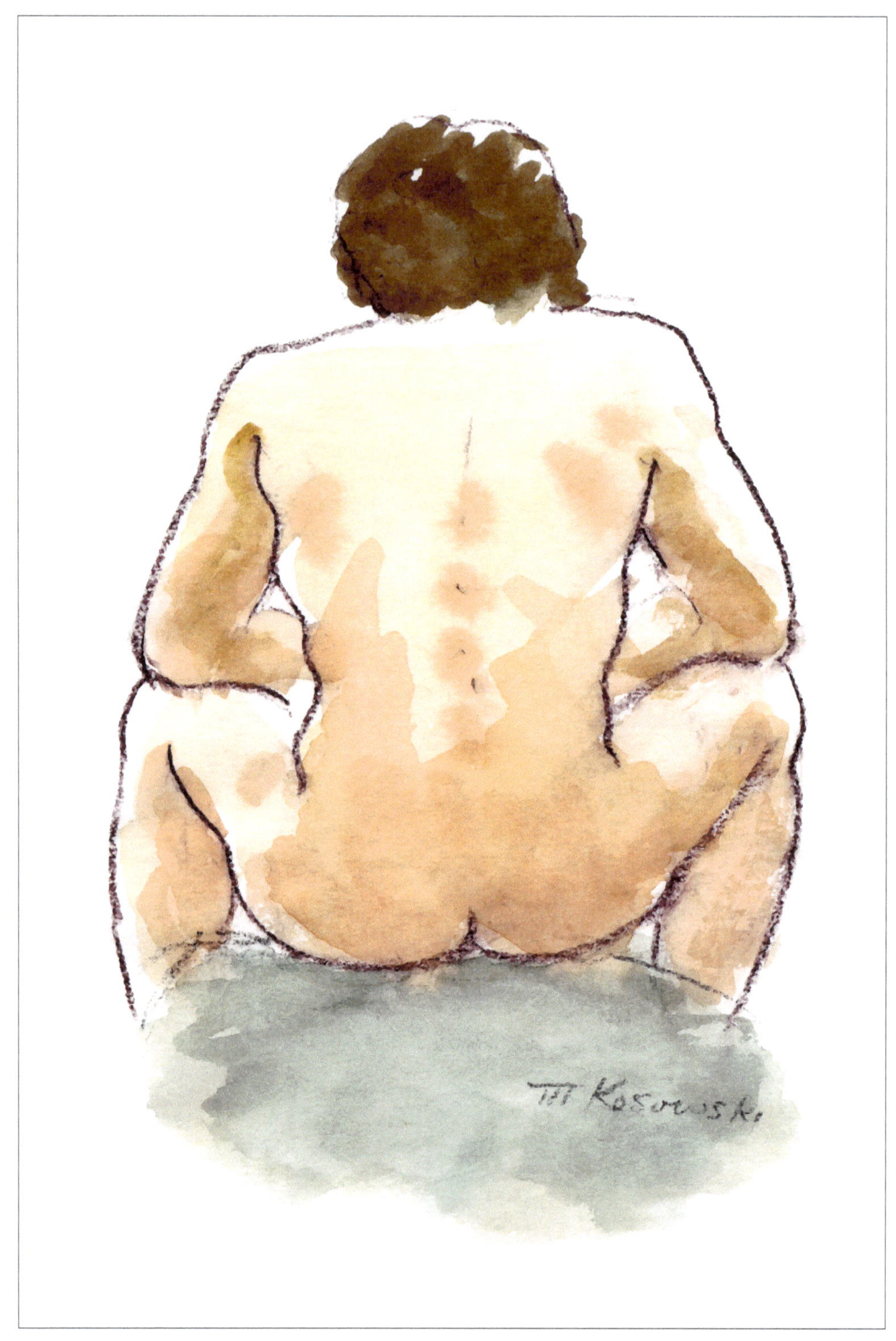
TM Kosowski

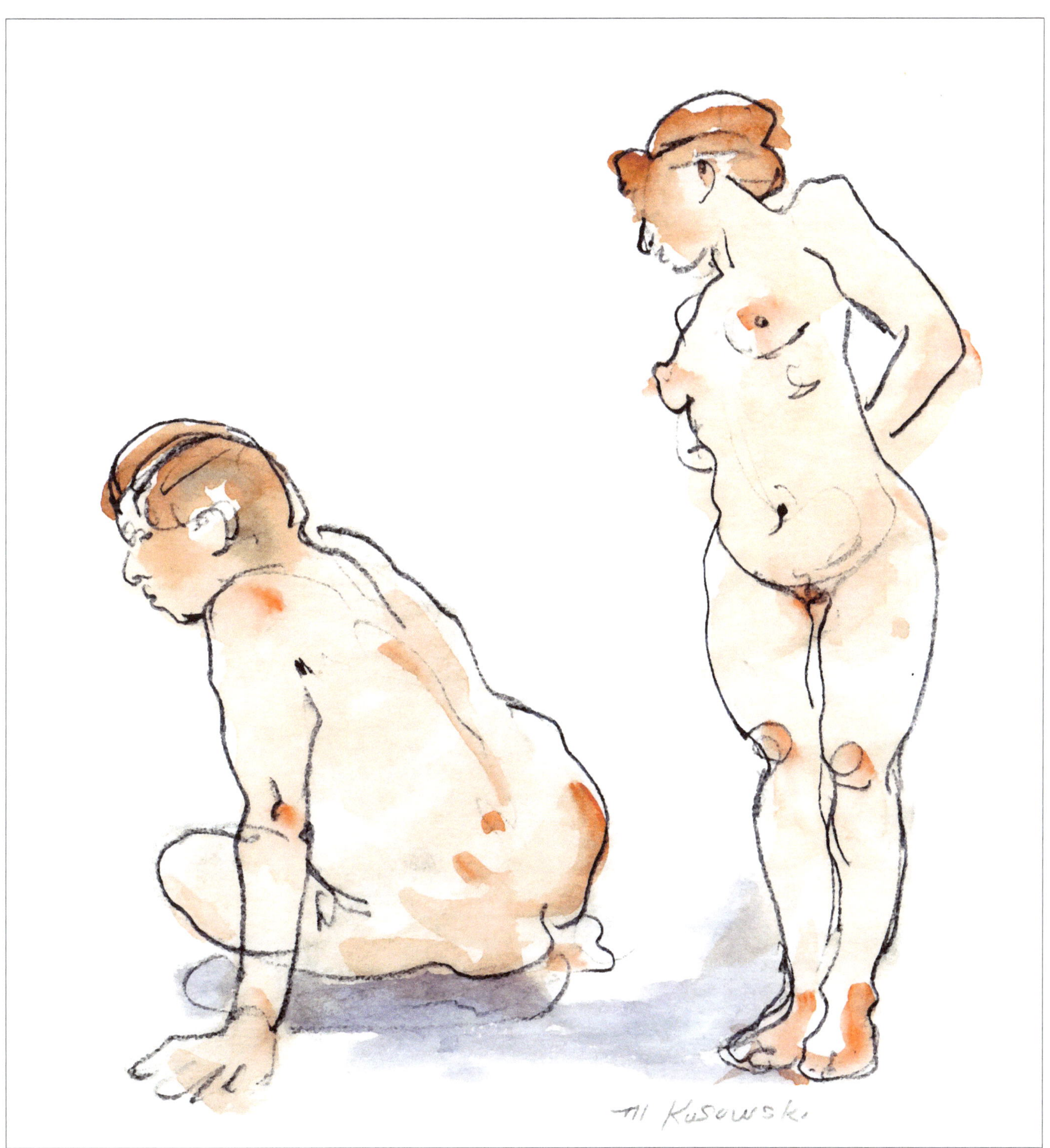
M Kosowski

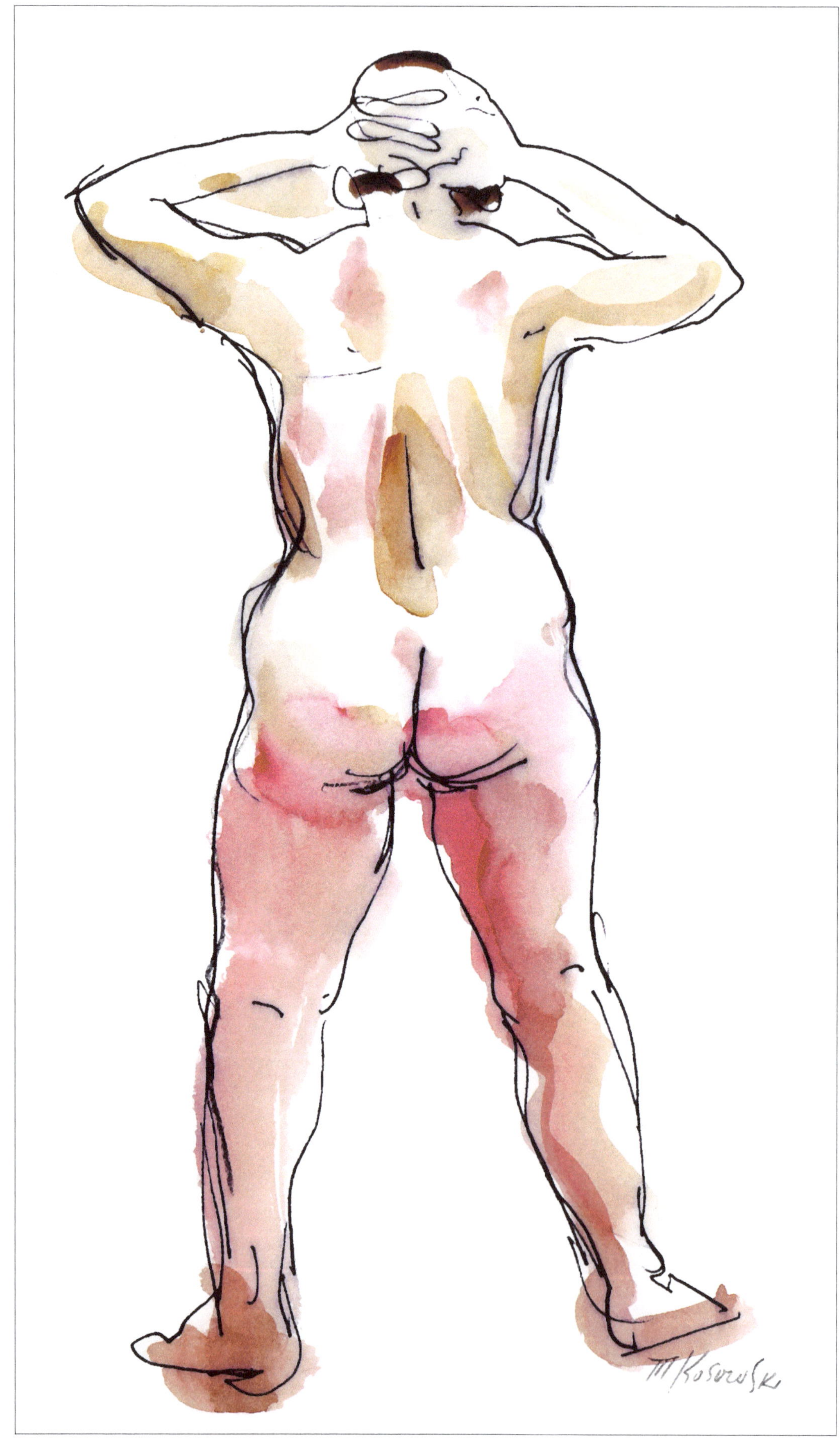

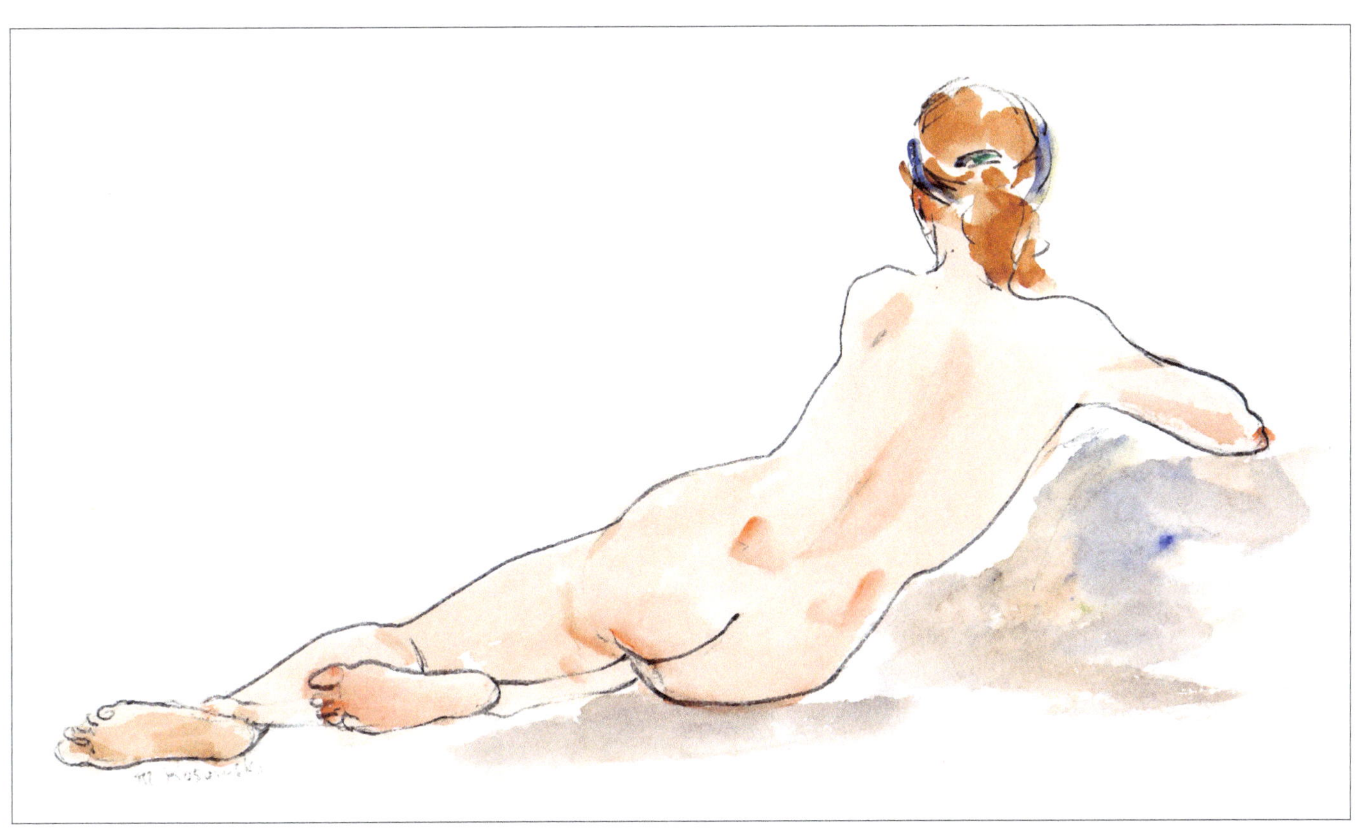

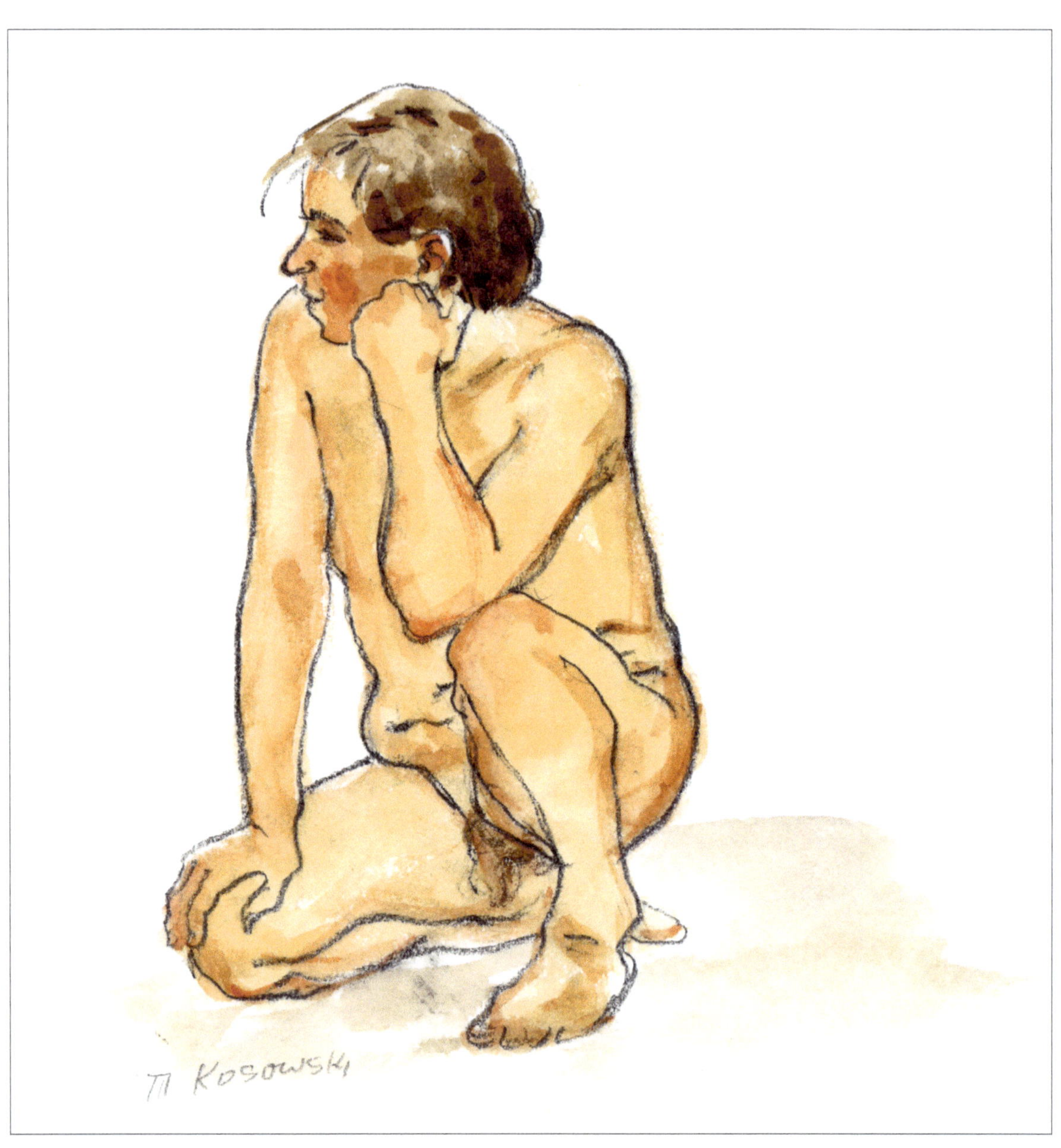
M KOSOWSKI

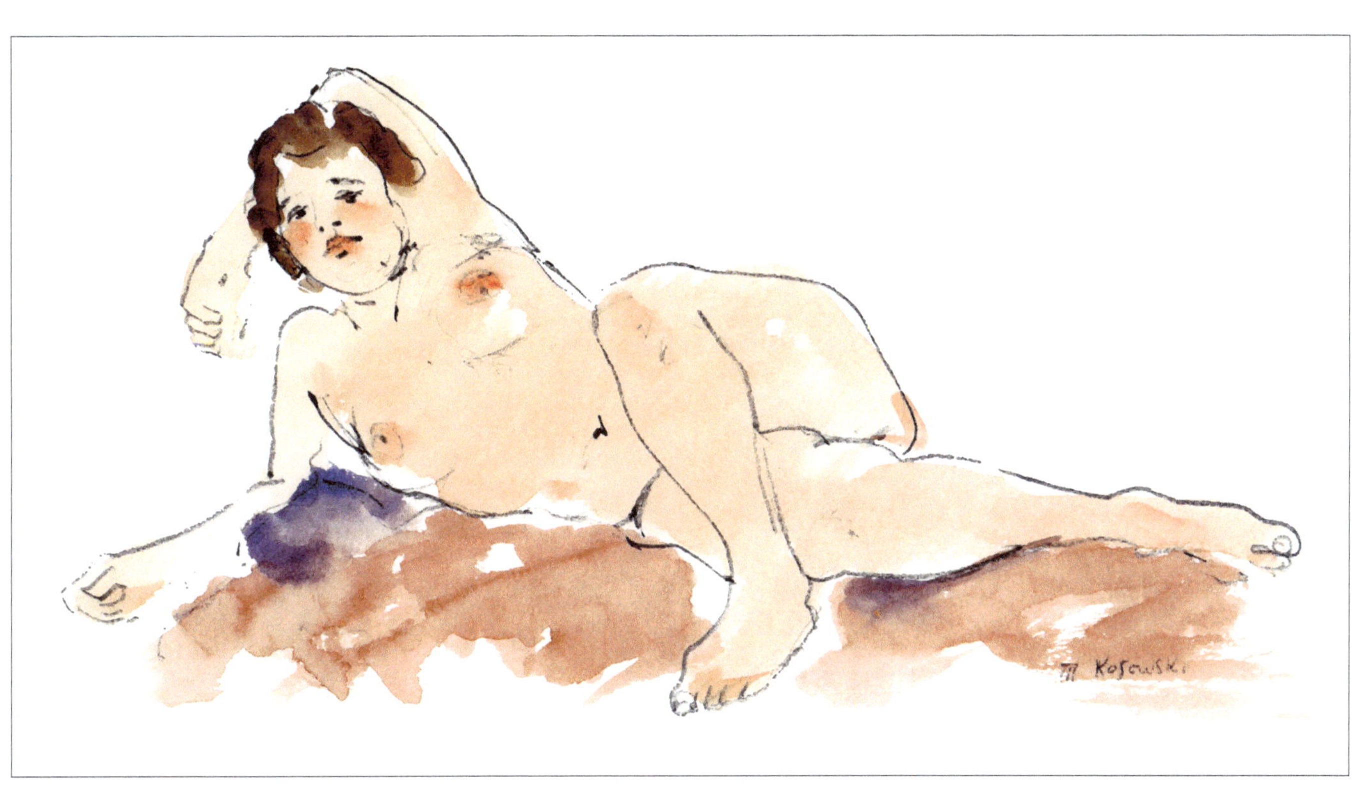
M Kosowski

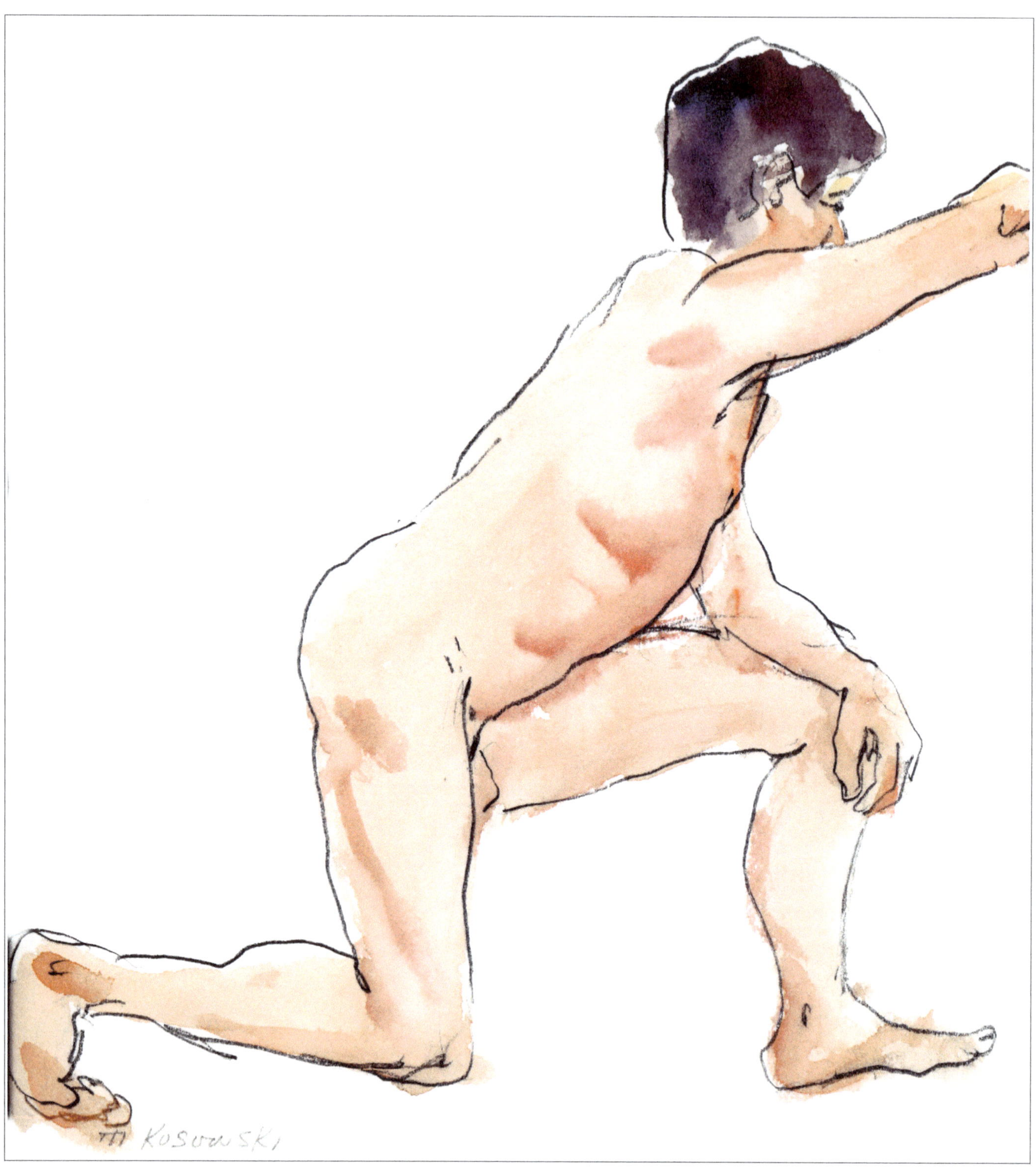
m KOSOWSKI

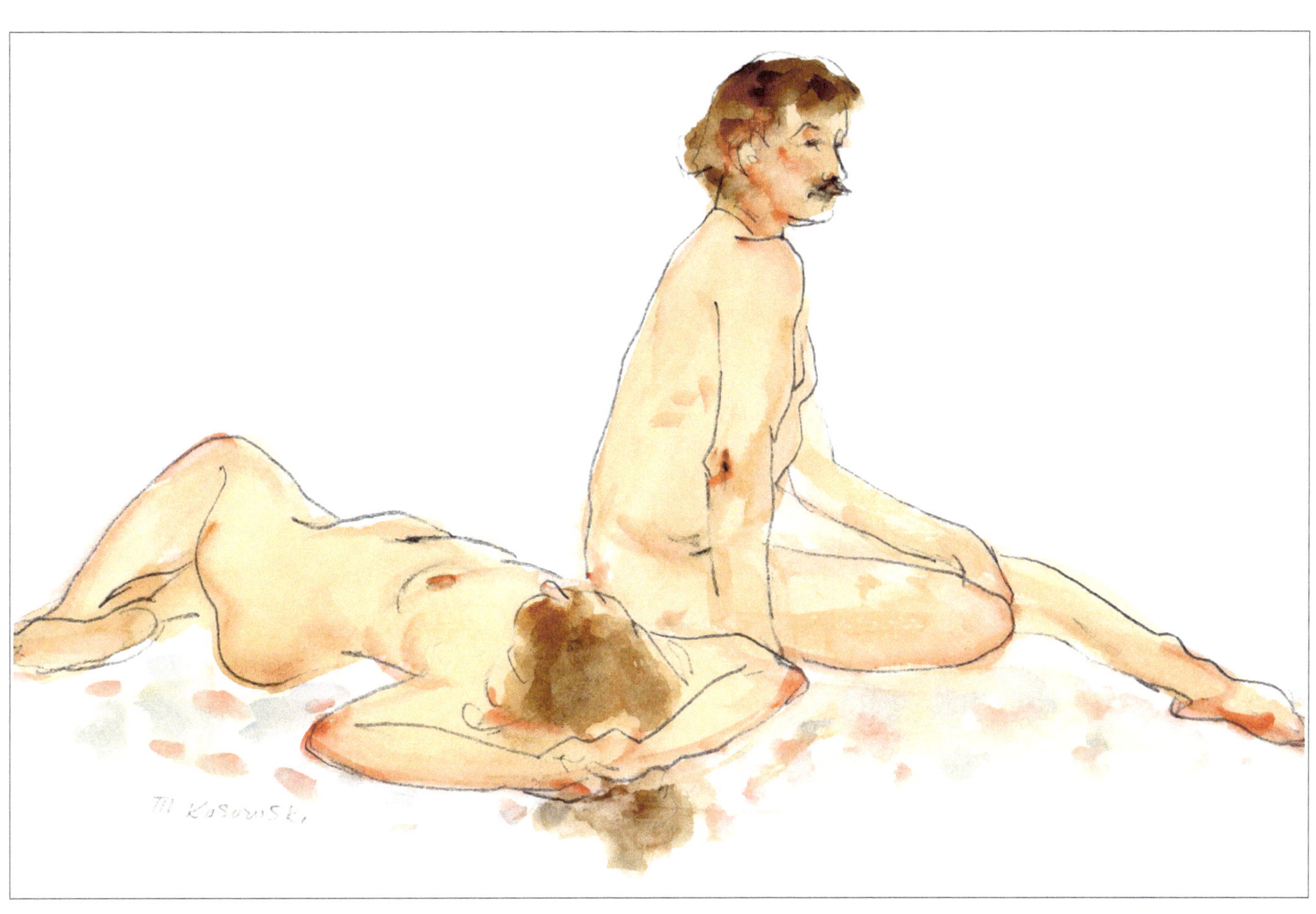

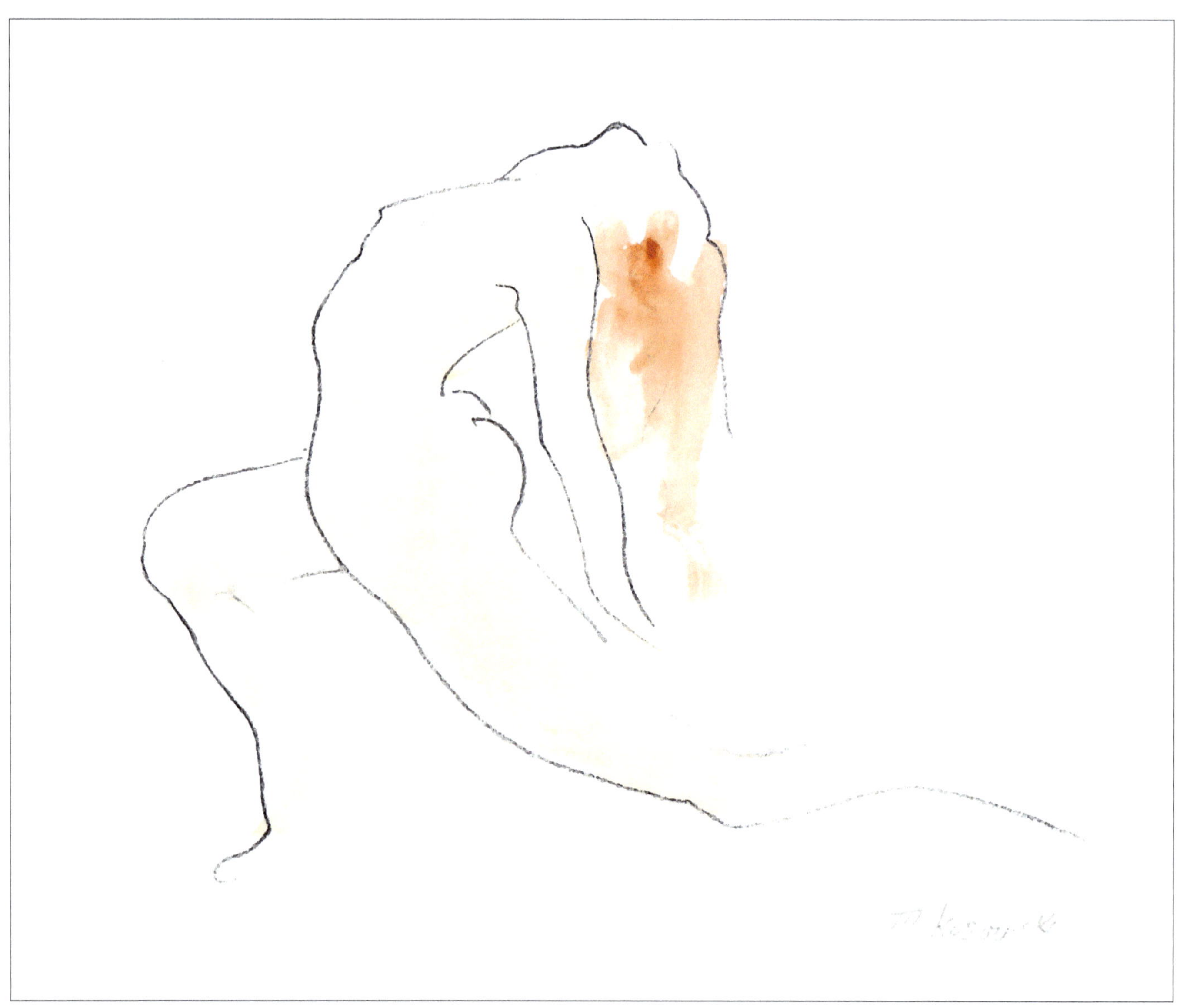

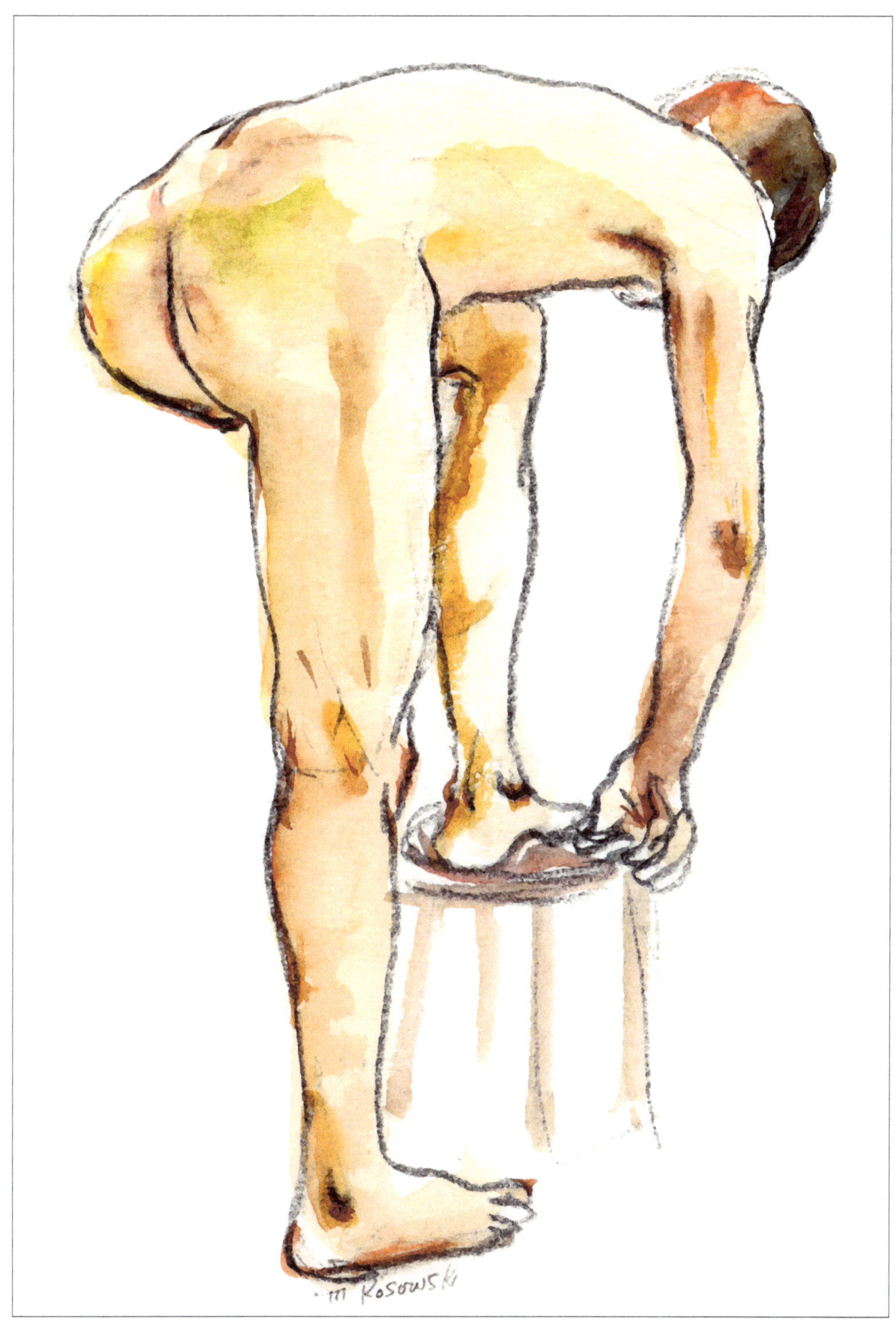
m Kosowski

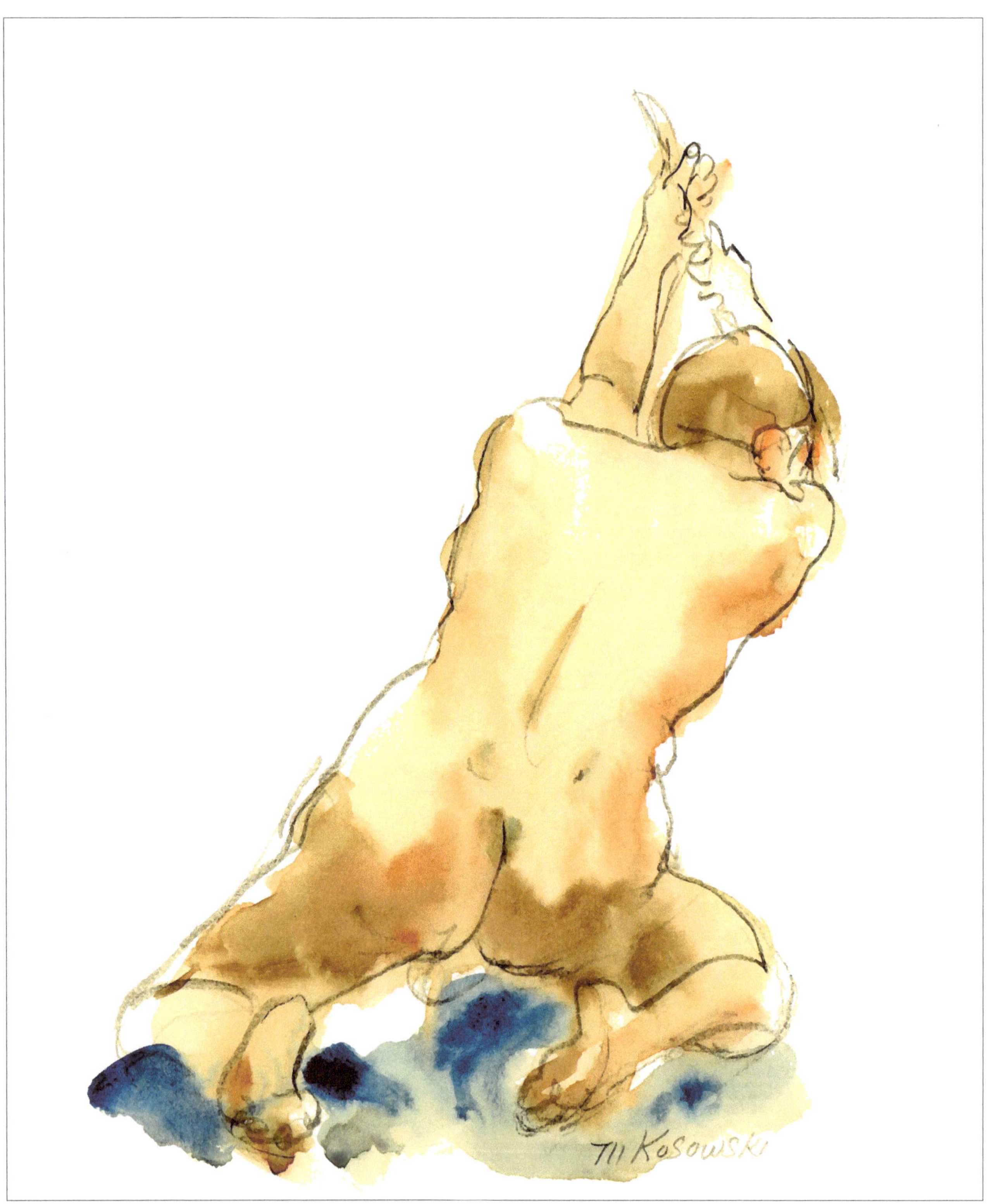
Kosowski

www.ingramcontent.com/pod-product-compliance
Lightning Source LLC
LaVergne TN
LVHW070133110826
845147LV00002B/244

9780615247014